Cambridge Elements ≡

Elements in the Problems of God
edited by
Michael L. Peterson
Asbury Theological Seminary

THE PROBLEM OF ANIMAL PAIN

Victoria Campbell
Global Methodist Church

CAMBRIDGE
UNIVERSITY PRESS

Shaftesbury Road, Cambridge CB2 8EA, United Kingdom

One Liberty Plaza, 20th Floor, New York, NY 10006, USA

477 Williamstown Road, Port Melbourne, VIC 3207, Australia

314–321, 3rd Floor, Plot 3, Splendor Forum, Jasola District Centre,
New Delhi – 110025, India

103 Penang Road, #05–06/07, Visioncrest Commercial, Singapore 238467

Cambridge University Press is part of Cambridge University Press & Assessment,
a department of the University of Cambridge.

We share the University's mission to contribute to society through the pursuit of
education, learning and research at the highest international levels of excellence.

www.cambridge.org
Information on this title: www.cambridge.org/9781009478663

DOI: 10.1017/9781009270717

First published 2023

A catalogue record for this publication is available from the British Library

ISBN 978-1-009-47866-3 Hardback
ISBN 978-1-009-27067-0 Paperback
ISSN 2754-8724 (online)
ISSN 2754-8716 (print)

Cambridge University Press & Assessment has no responsibility for the persistence
or accuracy of URLs for external or third-party internet websites referred to in this
publication and does not guarantee that any content on such websites is, or will
remain, accurate or appropriate.

The Problem of Animal Pain

Elements in the Problems of God

DOI: 10.1017/9781009270717
First published online: December 2023

Victoria Campbell
Global Methodist Church

Author for correspondence: Victoria Campbell,
victoriacampbell.tx@gmail.com

Abstract: In this Element, atheists cite animal pain as compelling evidence against the existence of the loving God portrayed in the Judeo-Christian Bible. William Rowe, Paul Draper, Richard Dawkins, and others claim widespread unnecessary suffering exists in nature and challenge theism with the evidential problem of natural evil. This Element engages the scientific literature in order to evaluate the validity of those claims and offers a theodicy of God's providential care for animals through natural pain-mitigating processes.

This Element also has a video abstract:
http://www.cambridge.org/problem-of-animal-pain

Keywords: animal pain, suffering, theodicy, evil, (Richard) Dawkins

ISBNs: 9781009478663 (HB), 9781009270670 (PB), 9781009270717 (OC)
ISSNs: 2754-8724 (online), 2754-8716 (print)

Contents

1 Animal Pain and the Evidential Problem of Natural Evil

Since the publication of Charles Darwin's *Origin of Species*, it has become increasingly clear that predation, pain, and death not only preceded human existence but have also been woven into the very fabric of life (Darwin 2009). With the acceptance of neo-Darwinian evolution in mainline science and recognition of pain and death in nature, theistic belief (specifically Judeo-Christian belief) has been challenged to explain creaturely suffering in a world created by a loving God. Unsurprisingly, a perception has grown that theism is incompatible with science and cannot justify natural processes that cause pain and biological death, often referred to as *natural evil*.

The disregard some theologians have shown toward animal pain has contributed to this perceived impotence of Judeo-Christian thought. However, the most significant reason theistic responses continue to lack strength is due to shallow abstract philosophical understandings of the natural world that do not consider empirical details of suffering to be important. Scientific literature on the perception of pain across species has rarely been engaged when countering atheists' arguments. Without more robust understandings of pain perception and natural ecosystems, atheists are able to depict the Judeo-Christian God as being either indifferent to suffering or another nonexistent deity in a pantheon of human gods. Consequently, nontheists have been able to claim that the existence of animal suffering and death well before the first human beings strengthens the *evidential problem of natural evil*.

1.1 The Problem of Evil

The philosophical problem of evil falls into two subproblems that employ different strategies: the *logical problem* and the *evidential problem* (Peterson et al. 2009: 145–154). A philosophical "problem" is an argument where the starting premises have credibility and the conclusion derived from those premises challenges the belief claims of their philosophical opponents.

The logical problem of evil argues the very strong claim that it is logically impossible for God and evil to coexist. The evidential problem of evil argues the weaker claim that evidence of evil in the world makes it unlikely God exists. The evils referred to in these problems fall into two broad categories: *moral evil* and *natural evil*. Moral evil is associated with wrongful or hurtful actions of either free human beings or other moral agents and can include acts such as murder, betrayal, theft, and attributes like dishonesty, cruelty, and greed. Natural evil encompasses physical suffering resulting from impersonal non-moral agents or processes in nature and can include pain and death caused by flood, fire, famine, disease, and disability.

1.2 The Evidential Problem of Natural Evil

In his 1979 essay, "The Problem of Evil and Some Varieties of Atheism," William Rowe argued against the existence of an omnipotent, omniscient, wholly good God as follows (336):

(1) There exist instances of intense suffering which an omnipotent, omniscient being could have prevented without thereby losing some greater good or permitting some evil equally bad or worse.

(2) An omniscient, wholly good being would prevent the occurrence of any intense suffering it could, unless it could not do so without thereby losing some greater good or permitting some evil equally bad or worse.

(3) There does not exist an omnipotent, omniscient, wholly good being.

Rowe's famous evidential problem of evil has been persuasive and widely cited throughout the philosophical literature. Critical engagement with Rowe's argument involves assessing and addressing its two premises. Premise (1) functions as an *evidential premise*, a statement of perceived facts, and premise (2) serves as a *theological premise*, describing God's purposes and values. Stating Rowe's claims more explicitly:

- There is widespread suffering in nature.
- There is unnecessary suffering in nature.
- God is purportedly an omniscient, omnipotent being.
- A wholly good omniscient, omnipotent being (God) would prevent widespread and unnecessary suffering.
- God has *not* prevented widespread, unnecessary suffering.
- Therefore, an omnipotent, omniscient wholly good God does not exist.

Rowe adds two potential *defeaters* to his argument that would undermine its strength against the existence of an omnipotent, omniscient wholly good God:

- If the prevention of suffering permitted an evil equally bad or worse.
- If the prevention of suffering permitted the loss of a greater good.

For the purposes of this inquiry, the adjective "intense" will be set aside since all suffering is subjective and unquantifiable. Consequently, Rowe's argument will be evaluated by simply considering whether there is unnecessary suffering in nature.

In evidential premise (1) of Rowe's argument, suffering is cited as evidence that makes the nonexistence of God a reasonable conclusion that is "more probable than not." Rowe's essay cites natural evil as having particularly negative evidential bearing against theistic belief. As support for premise (1),

Rowe describes a fawn trapped in a forest fire dying a protracted, agonizing death (1979: 337). The case of "Bambi," as it is often called, purportedly typifies the many evils occurring daily in the natural world. Rowe's essential thrust is not the logical impossibility of theism being compatible with evil, but theism is improbable given evidence of evil. The important evidential premise (1) in the Rowe-type argument is supported by a variety of presumably factual claims about nonhuman suffering caused by natural processes like forest fires, predation, parasitism, disease, famine, or instances of what appear to be acts of animal cruelty against other animals. Such claims suggest the amount of suffering in the world has not been minimized and is instead alarmingly high. Nevertheless, while there is agreement that natural processes can cause injury to creatures' tissues, a central associated quandary lies in whether creatures with injured tissues perceive pain identically across species. For this reason, the science behind pain perception should be a major consideration when evaluating the problem of creaturely suffering.

In theological premise (2) of Rowe's argument, God's priorities are implicitly assumed to include the prevention of pain and discomfort throughout creation, a position that may be called *hedonistic utilitarianism* for our purposes.

1.3 Indifferent Universe or Loving Judeo-Christian God?

Joining Rowe in thinking unnecessary suffering in nature is excessive, Paul Draper cites biological failure as additional support for the evidential premise regarding natural evil and makes the theological claim "a morally perfect God would strongly prefer that every sentient being flourish for a significant portion of their lives" (2007). He also takes a *hedonistic utilitarian* approach to argue a wholly good God's goal would be to minimize suffering and maximize the biological success and pleasure of creatures (1989: 334–337). However, do Rowe's and Draper's theological claims adequately reflect either a fair biblical interpretation or theological understanding of the Judeo-Christian worldview? Early on, their theological starting assumptions appear to be based upon the materialistic and hedonistic utilitarian value systems of many nontheistic philosophers, not the love-oriented ethic associated with the Judeo-Christian God (Deut 6:5; Lev 19:18b; Matt 22:36–40; John 14:23–24; 15:12–13; Rom 12:9–17; 1 John 4:7–12; 1 Cor 13:1–7).

Adopting a similar depiction of God as Rowe, Draper claims a morally perfect, omnipotent, omniscient God (1989: 336–337):

- Could create goal-oriented creatures (including humans) without biologically necessary pain systems.
- Would maximize pleasure and minimize pain except when morally necessary.

Draper further argues the hypothesis of indifference (the atheistic worldview of an indifferent universe unconcerned with creaturely pleasure and pain) is more probable than the hypothesis of theism (the conceptual core of the Judeo-Christian worldview that revolves around God's love for creatures). Draper's hypothesis of indifference states "neither the nature nor the condition of sentient beings on earth is the result of benevolent or malevolent actions performed by non-human persons" (1989: 332). Other philosophers concur: "The hypothesis of indifference predicts the data of an apparently indifferent universe" (Tooley 2019: 48).

This argument strategy is known as abductive reasoning, also called *inference to the best explanation*. Inference to the best explanation is an evaluative procedure that weighs competing hypotheses against each other and is a familiar pattern of scientific reasoning. In such evaluations, the "best explanation" is usually determined by the hypothesis – or philosophical perspective in this case – that successfully encompasses the widest range of empirical evidence, has the greatest explanatory and predictive power, and thereby has the ability to correctly anticipate outcomes. Consequently, when considering the evidential problem of natural evil, inference to the best explanation can compare the relative explanatory power of the Judeo-Christian and atheistic worldviews.

Rowe suggests theists must be scientifically uninformed in order to believe in God, calling this point of view "friendly atheism" and asserting theists would not be rationally justified in holding to theism if they were better acquainted with the findings of science (1979: 340). While it is true a better assessment of the problem of pain will be obtained if the findings of science are incorporated into the reasoning process, it is still an open question whether atheism has more explanatory power than the Judeo-Christian worldview. It is possible Rowe and Draper's statements regarding evidence of pain in the world may, upon interaction with the scientific literature, be impressionistic at best.

2 Theistic Responses to Animal Suffering

Theistic responses to the evidential problem of natural evil have included defenses and theodicies. A *defense* attempts to show the existence of God is not logically incompatible with the existence of evil. A *theodicy* provides a framework that supports God's benevolence by explaining how the evil encountered is part of some larger good.

Theists have attempted to protect God from the problem of creaturely suffering by undermining claims that typically support Rowe's evidential and theological premises. One general approach has been to diminish the strength of evidential premise (1) – *an omnipotent, omniscient being could have prevented unnecessary suffering without thereby losing some greater good or permitting some evil equally bad or worse* – by treating animals as either theologically insignificant to God or ignoring credible evidence of their pain. Another approach addresses premise (1) by suggesting pain is an unfortunate but necessary product of the universe's ordered regularity. However, most responses have sought to undermine the strength of theological premise (2) – *an omniscient, wholly good being would prevent the occurrence of any suffering it could, unless it could not do so without thereby losing some greater good or permitting some evil equally bad or worse* – by either maintaining God's goodness while limiting God's omniscience and/or omnipotence, or by claiming suffering in creation is necessary for the punishment or promotion of moral agents.

2.1 Cartesian/Neo-Cartesian Defenses

Cartesian/Neo-Cartesian defenses argue animal suffering is either theologically insignificant to God or there is no credible evidence of animal pain. These approaches aim to weaken claims that animal suffering diminishes the probable existence of a wholly good omnipotent God.

The notion that animal suffering is theologically unimportant to God goes back to St. Augustine of Hippo (ca. 400 CE), who employed Stoic philosophical assumptions, not Scripture, to dismiss the suffering of animals (Moritz 2014: 351). According to Augustine, animal suffering is real but theologically insignificant because animals do not have souls; souls make suffering meaningful, thus God only cares about the suffering of ensouled humans.

René Descartes developed the more modern Cartesian view of animal suffering which claims animals do not have self-conscious awareness and therefore cannot experience morally significant pain (Murray 2011: 41–72; Dougherty 2014: 56–95). Descartes believed animals were *insentient* machine-like organisms lacking the cognitive capacity to perceive pain, so their distressed responses were morally insignificant.

In contrast to the Cartesian view, neo-Cartesian approaches acknowledge animals are *sentient*, yet claim animals lack some other aspect of human character that enables creatures' experiences to be considered meaningful suffering (Harrison 1989: 83–84; Adams 1999: 28; Lewis 2001: 135–136; Hick 2010: 309–314). However, while scholars could once claim "no strict argument can be mounted for or against the existence of animal pain" (Harrison 1989: 81), Trent Dougherty correctly observes such claims are no longer tenable in light of publications like the 2009 U.S. National Academy of Sciences' *Recognition and Alleviation of Pain in Laboratory Animals* (Dougherty 2014: 61–64).

The Cartesian/neo-Cartesian line of reasoning, which claims *no* nonhuman animals can perceive pain in a theologically meaningful way, has several serious weaknesses. First, claims nonhuman animals are incapable of feeling pain have been speculative rather than empirically based and are now easily defeated by scientific research. Second, statements suggesting animals are theologically unimportant to God undermine Scriptures that depict God's concern for all creatures, providing them food when they are hungry and watching over them even as they give birth (Gen 1:20–25, 30–31; Job 38:39–39:4; Ps 136:25; 145:15–16).

In short, *Cartesian/neo-Cartesian defenses* have the following strengths as they:

- Affirm the omnipotence and omniscience of God.
- Protect God from the claim God allows animals to suffer.

However, *Cartesian/neo-Cartesian defenses* also have the following weaknesses as they:

- Take an anthropocentric worldview that diminishes the theological significance of other living creatures in creation.
- Take a theologically speculative position that is not well supported by Scripture.
- Take a scientifically indefensible position that there are *no* animals that can perceive pain despite contemporary scientific research strongly supporting pain perception in more highly evolved animals.

2.2 Natural Order Defenses

Natural order defenses argue pain is a necessary and inevitable aspect of the well-ordered universe God created. Proponents of this approach have tended to be scientist-theologians and include John Polkinghorne, Holmes Rolston III, and Arthur Peacocke.

Polkinghorne depicted the universe as bearing the divine gift of self-making fruitfulness where creation participates in its own creating, yet occasionally results in blind alleys and death (2010: 556). Rolston understood the dynamic nature of healthy ecosystems where advanced sentient life only emerges in species higher on the food chain and death is a necessary part of the cycle of life where nothing goes to waste (1987: 136). Peacocke noted pain and suffering are the complementary opposites of pleasure and well-being that come with a creature's emergent consciousness and are necessary for responsiveness to the surrounding environment and continued survival (1993: 68).

Natural order defenses provide a big picture view of how order and regularity in nature benefit a biologically diverse and dynamic creation. Yet, they also paint a portrait of individual creatures who each suffer alone for the greater good of evolutionary processes that they cannot comprehend. This approach can convey a God who is indifferent to the suffering of creatures caught in these processes, as though good ends for the greater creation are sufficient to justify the difficult means endured by the individual creature: a very utilitarian view of God's value system.

Natural order defenses weaken Rowe's evidential premise (1) by arguing pain is a *necessary* component for survival and the absence of pain and death would permit the equally bad or worse evil of nonexistence. The strengths of natural order defenses are they:

- Appeal to natural laws widely accepted in science.
- Emphasize empirically observable benefits of order and regularity in the cosmos.
- Note the advantages of dynamic over static ecosystems.
- Lessen notions of wastefulness in nature.
- Point to empirically observable life/death/life cycles found in nature.
- Recognize the death of one creature creates opportunity for life of another.
- Recognize the same neurocognitive ability to perceive pain enables a creature to perceive pleasure.
- Observe pain is necessary for creatures' survival.

Natural order defenses also have weaknesses as they:

- Lack a compassionate approach to the suffering of the individual creature.
- Do not incorporate pain mitigation strategies found in nature.

2.3 Process Theism and Kenosis Approaches

To defend God's goodness in a creation where natural processes cause pain and death, some theologians have removed God's responsibility for suffering by undermining God's omniscience and omnipotence either directly or indirectly. Process theologians taking this nonstandard approach argue God does not have the power to prevent suffering (Griffin 1981: 105; Hartshorne 1984; Buckareff 2000; Pinnock 2001; Viney 2018). God's power over nature is purportedly limited to the power of love to persuade, not power that controls (Barbour 1997: 326–327; McDaniel 1998: 167). They further claim God has no fore-knowledge of events, thus God cannot know what will happen until it happens (McDaniel 1998: 164). Under these assumptions, process theists affirm God is

wholly good as they claim suffering exists because God is incapable of prevent-
ing it.

While successfully affirming God's goodness, this approach has several
weaknesses. Besides abandoning classical Christian doctrines on God's omniscience and omnipotence (Oden 1992: 48–53), it lacks scriptural support for its
position while ignoring these divine attributes in the biblical text. God's omniscience is supported by Hebrews 4:13: "Nothing in all creation is hidden from
God's sight." God's vast foreknowledge is proclaimed in passages like Isaiah
46:10: "I make known the end from the beginning, from ancient times, what is
still to come." The biblical text not only supports God's active power over
nature (Psalm 147:8–9, 15–18), but also includes more unusual interventions
such as when God parted the Red Sea (Exodus 14) and Jesus calmed the storm
(Mark 4:35–41). Consequently, process theism's claims tend to be theologically
speculative without support from either traditional Christian reasoning or
Scripture. Moreover, this depiction presents a God who is powerless to prevent
suffering and leaves "a greater problem of evil and suffering, not a lesser one,
since there is no clear end to evil" (Sollereder 2019: 66).

Besides lacking power to prevent harm, if God lacks foreknowledge, it
suggests either: (1) God had no idea the creation set in place would eventually
produce disease, pain, and death, or (2) it was a risk God was willing to take.
Ultimately, process theism offers a weak defense, depicting a world of suffering
created by a kind but powerless God who should not be blamed for what he
could not foresee.

In contrast, kenosis approaches are more robust than process theism because
they deny neither God's omniscience, omnipotence, nor God's ability to act in
the world (Polkinghorne 2001). Kenosis makes the weaker, more defensible
claim that God *chooses* to lay down power in many circumstances rather than
the stronger process theism claim that God's power is limited. In doing so,
kenosis approaches are compatible with both scriptural depictions and classical
Christian doctrines of God's foreknowledge and power as well as God's even-
tual triumph of good over evil.

Yet, kenosis does not explain why God allows animal suffering. While it can
be argued God sets aside power so moral agents like humans might gain moral
or spiritual insight from suffering, this is harder to justify in the case of nonhumans. Furthermore, "while kenosis may explain the origin of suffering, it does
not – by itself – offer hope to individuals who suffer" (Sollereder 2019: 72).
Although proponents of kenosis claim God shares each creature's suffering,
Ruth Page objects: "God has merely changed from a powerful onlooker to
a suffering onlooker, and creation remains on its own" (Rolston 1987: 144–146;
Page 1996: 53; McDaniel 1998: 165–166; Peacocke 2001: 37–39).

In summary, the strengths of *process theism approaches* are they:

- Acknowledge the existence of animal pain is credible and animals are theologically significant to God.
- Affirm the loving-kindness of a wholly good God.

The weaknesses of *process theism approaches* are they:

- Reject God's omnipotence, omniscience, and responsibility for suffering in the created order.
- Depict a God who is powerless to stop evil and offers little support to creatures that suffer.
- Lack scriptural support for their claims while ignoring biblical texts that depict God's omnipotence, omniscience, and power to defeat evil.

The strengths of *kenosis approaches* are they:

- Acknowledge the existence of animal pain is credible and animals are theologically significant to God.
- Affirm the loving-kindness of a wholly good God.
- Acknowledge God's omnipotence, omniscience, and responsibility for suffering in the created order.
- Affirm God's power to overcome and defeat evil.
- Depict a God who suffers alongside creatures.

The weaknesses of *kenosis approaches* are they:

- Depict a God who has inexplicably chosen to lay aside the power to intervene and alleviate suffering in nature.
- Offer no succor to creatures that suffer.

2.4 Suffering as Punishment: The Theodicy of Adam's Fall

A more traditional explanation for suffering has been to claim it is justified punishment for Adam and Eve's sin. In Western thought, theologians followed Augustine, assuming Genesis 1–3 intended to describe the origins of the material universe, pain, and biological death. In order to exonerate God for the existence of the latter two maladies, many Western theologians regarded suffering as punishment for sin imposed upon humans and animals alike after the Fall. According to Augustine (1982: 2:164–165), "Death occurred on the day when our first parents did what God had forbidden. ... When Adam and Eve, therefore, lost their privileged state, their bodies became subject to disease and death, like the bodies of animals."

John Calvin expanded on Augustine's thought, blaming the punishment of Adam and Eve for the suffering of all creatures (1849: Romans 8:20–22):

> It is then indeed meet for us to consider what a dreadful curse we have deserved, since all created things in themselves blameless, both on earth and in the visible heaven, undergo punishment for our sins; for it has not happened through their own fault, that they are liable to corruption. Thus the condemnation of mankind is imprinted on the heavens, and on the earth, and on all creatures.

This belief became pervasive in the Western church and successfully absolved God from responsibility for creaturely suffering, laying that burden on human beings instead.

2.4.1 Greco-Roman Ideas Imposed upon the Ancient Mesopotamian Genesis Text

More recent scholarship indicates Genesis 1–11 was shaped by ancient Mesopotamian thought (Jacobsen 1981; Walton 1990, 2018; Hess and Tsumura 1994; Chavalas and Younger 2002; Arnold and Strawn 2016). This is unsurprising since the text itself along with recent geographical and geological research places Genesis 1–11 in the Mesopotamian Tigris-Euphrates valley (Gen 2:10–14; 10:8–12; 11:1–4, 27–31; Sauer 1996; Hill 2000).

Since Genesis 5, 11, and Abram's birth in 2166 BCE place Adam's era around 4000 BCE, Augustine – a resident of Hippo in Roman-controlled North Africa approximately 4,400 years later – would have been at a great disadvantage interpreting this text because his Greco-Roman worldview would not have been in alignment with ancient Mesopotamian thought. Importantly, many Mesopotamian theological concepts and symbols found in Genesis 1–3 were foreign to gentile influencers of the early church like Augustine.

Jean Delumeau, a French historian who studied the Catholic Church, explained the profound impact Greco-Roman myths had upon church fathers as they interpreted the Garden of Eden account and created an influential new genre of literature known as the *Hexaemeron* (2000: 6–21). In "The Influence of Greek Philosophy on the Early Commentaries on Genesis", Greek professor Frank Robbins documented how the Hexaemeral writers were consciously and unconsciously shaped by the Greco-Roman philosophy and science of their day (1912: 219). Plato's *Timaeus* had an immense influence in framing their worldview, creating "a Platonic principle that God cannot be the cause of anything evil" (221–222). A logical result of this principle was God could not be culpable for any tribulations found in the world: "Nor would our writers admit that God is the cause of the harm done by animals, poisonous plants and reptiles, or thorns;

they escape all these difficulties by saying that man's sin was the cause of all" (222). There are consequently sound reasons for suspecting pagan philosophical views created an intellectual milieu that diverted responsibility for pain and death in creation from God to the shoulders of humankind.

Furthermore, if the author(s) of Genesis wished to declare Adam and Eve were responsible for all sin, pain, and death in the created order, one might expect this theme to be expounded elsewhere in the Torah. Yet, the Jewish writers of the Old Testament hardly mention Adam and Eve at all and did *not* view them as the source of human sin, pain, or biological death (Wiley 2002: 28–35; Green 2017). Rather, the Fall as the origin of all human sin and suffering does not appear to have surfaced until after the Hellenization of Jewish lands (ca. 200 BCE–100 CE; Witherington 2006: 32–35). This may explain the remarkable resemblance between Hesiod's etiological myth *Pandora's Jar*, which was the Greek pagans' explanation of the origins of human suffering (ca. 750–650 BCE), and the subsequent fallen view of Adam and Eve found in later noncanonical writings dating from the second century BCE to the early second century CE: *Life of Adam and Eve (Apocalypse of Moses), 4 Ezra, 2 Baruch, Biblical Antiquities, Sirach 25:24*, and *Wisdom of Solomon 2:23–24* (Wiley 2002: 33–34; Hesiod 2008: 39–40; Green 2017: 100–105).

However, Hellenized thinkers using Genesis 2–3 to depict an invasion of physical illness and biological death into God's perfect world would not have understood the broader theological implications of the term "death" in the Jewish worldview. As Old Testament professor Hans Walter Wolff explains, the Hebrew Bible views the living and dead as more than biological states of existence. Those terms have theological implications where the "living" are those who praise God in both word and deed whereas the "dead" represent those who have broken relationship with God and "have been expelled from Yahweh's sphere of influence" (Wolff 1981: 106–110).

This significant insight into the Jewish worldview assists when interpreting the competing claims of God and the serpent in the garden (Gen 2:16–17; 3:4–5 NIV).

> [16]And the Lord God commanded the man, "You are free to eat from any tree in the garden; [17]but you must not eat from the tree of the knowledge of good and evil, for when you eat from it you will certainly die."
>
> [4]"You will not certainly die," the serpent said to the woman. [5]"For God knows that when you eat from it your eyes will be opened, and you will be like God, knowing good and evil."

Whereas God was likely talking about relational death where a person rejects a right relationship with God, the snake appears to define death as merely biological. By using a different definition of "death," the serpent duplicitously yet truthfully claimed the humans would not die biologically on the day they disobeyed God (von Rad 1961: 87; Blocher 1984: 139; Arnold 2013: 65–66). However, the serpent did *not* tell the humans their relationship with God would "die" as God had warned and result in their expulsion from sacred space (Moberly 1988: 16–18; Wenham 1994: 404; 2014: 74–75). Here, both the serpent and God speak the truth even as the passage reveals there is more to life and death than just a heartbeat. Interpreting "death" as rejection of God is also probable since the rest of the Old Testament teaches people about the importance of embracing God's wisdom so that they can "live" in right relationship with God and one another. Therefore, the most probable focus of this story was relational life or death with God, not the origins of biological death in nature.

2.4.2 ANE Paradigms Reveal God's Providential Care of Creation in Genesis 1

Besides revealing the intellectual biases of Augustine's day, research shows ancient Near Eastern (ANE) studies provide opportunities for alternate interpretations of Genesis unavailable to Augustine's worldview. Old Testament scholar John Walton explains the ancient Mesopotamian worldview prioritized the *order* and *function* of creation more than the *materials* forming creation (2009: 21–26; 2011: 139–152; Wolde 2015: 166). Consequently, Mesopotamians would recognize Gen 1:3–2:3 as a depiction of the ordering and inauguration of God's *cosmic temple* (Walton 2009: 53–85; 2011: 100–110; Lam 2010: 3–5; Wolde 2015: 162–163).

Days 1 (TIME), 2 (WATERS), and 3 (LAND and PLANTS) would be associated with the three functional spaces of the temple necessary to provide sustenance for all creatures (Walton 2009: 53–61; 2011: 152–171):

TIME + WATERS = SEASONS (cycles of rainfall and river inundation)

SEASONS + LAND + PLANTS = FOOD

Days 4–6 would be recognized as the installment of functionaries into their appropriate functional spaces (2009: 62–70; 2011: 172–178):

Day 4 = installs sun, moon, stars to mark day, night, and seasons in TIME

Day 5 = installs birds and fish in WATERS above (skies) and below (lakes/seas)

Day 6 = installs animals, men and women in LAND

Once these functional spaces were established and ordered, everything necessary for life was prepared and sustained in God's care (Day 7).

In the ancient Mesopotamian worldview, Genesis 1 depicts all creatures being given shelter and sustenance within God's cosmic temple – with no creature left on the outside, signifying all are in relationship with and cared for by God. This concept is encapsulated by the Jewish notion of *divine providence*, signifying "God's control and guidance of the universe and all it contains" (Birnbaum 1975: 172–173):

> Psalm 145 celebrates God's providential care for all his creation, declaring that "the Lord is good to all, his mercy is over all his works ... [. . .] The eyes of all look hopefully to thee, and thou givest them their food in due season. Thou openest thy hand, and satisfiest every living thing with favor."

The ANE cosmic temple interpretation of Genesis 1 is also significant because it undermines claims suggesting God is indifferent to the suffering of human and nonhuman creatures. From the Jewish perspective, a creature can only be "expelled from Yahweh's sphere of influence" by breaking relationship with God. Since only humans use their free will to break relationship with God as in the Garden (Genesis 3), it becomes difficult to explain how animals would become separated from God's providential care.

2.4.3 Consequences of Augustine's Linguistic Limitations in Genesis 2–3

Other difficulties complicated Augustine's interpretation of Genesis, including his inability to read it in its original language: Hebrew. According to Augustine's translator, John Hammond Taylor, Augustine never learned Hebrew and his Greek was almost nonexistent in 401 CE when he began his Genesis commentary, meaning his interpretations were based upon the Old Latin translation of the Greek Septuagint, not the original Hebrew text (Augustine 1982: 1:5). This becomes significant because the Greek Septuagint and Latin Vulgate both frequently translate the Hebrew *hā-'ādām* in Genesis 2–3 as a proper name, Adam. Yet, *hā-* is the definite article that means "the," so *hā-'ādām* should have been translated as "the man," "the human," or "the mortal" until the proper names Adam and Eve are used in Gen 3:17 and 3:20 (Hamilton 1990: 159–160; Middleton 2017: 73). Therefore, Augustine was unaware Genesis 2–3 may intentionally refer to a generic *archetypal* man and woman in order to convey a universal theological message to *all* human beings (Venema and McKnight 2017: 152). In other words, the goal may have been to pass down a cautionary tale to every human being that any one of us could be:

- *The serpent* – representing *usurpation* by rejecting God's authority and wisdom and replacing it with our own (Gen 2:16–17; 3:1–5)

- *The woman* – representing *syncretism* by compromising God's wisdom and blending it with false teachings (Gen 2:16–17; 3:2–3)
- *The man* – representing *disobedience* by acting on false teaching even though knowing to do so is contrary to God's wisdom (Gen 2:16–17; 3:6)

Although the interpretations offered here are not the only ways to read Genesis 1–3, they demonstrate that pertinent ANE information originally unavailable to Augustine can make alternative interpretations both viable and insightful when combined with other scholars' evaluations and critiques of the Fall narrative (Osborn 2014: 25–121; Venema and McKnight 2017: 111–191; Sollereder 2019: 13–43).

It should also be observed that the ANE interpretations of Genesis 1–3 offered here do *not* make scientifically untenable assertions that cause Judeo-Christian belief to seem irrational and/or improbable. Claims that the text describes the onset of pain and biological death in Earth's history subsequently disappear along with their conflicts with science (Miller 2007; Poinar and Poinar 2008; Darwin 2009; Venema and McKnight 2017). Therefore, it is essential to realize purported disagreements between Genesis 1–3 and science have been caused by textual interpretations derived from Greco-Roman intellectual foundations rather than ANE paradigms.

The theodicy of Adam's Fall claims suffering in creation is the deserved consequence of Adam and Eve's sin, deflecting responsibility for creaturely suffering and death away from God and placing blame on human beings instead.

The strengths of the *Fall theodicy* are:

- It is the basis of a widely accepted theological worldview among Western Christians and scholars for over 1,500 years.
- It offers a theological explanation for pain and death experienced by humans and nonhumans in the created order.
- It appears to acknowledge God's omnipotence, omniscience, and power over nature.
- It depicts a God who punishes evil and will ultimately end suffering and death.

The weaknesses of this theodicy are:

- This understanding of Genesis 1–3 is heavily dependent upon a Greco-Roman worldview rather than the Jewish and ANE milieu of the original text.
- It does not offer a strong explanation for why animals should be punished with pain and death for Adam and Eve's sin.

- It depicts a God who is indifferent to the suffering of nonhuman animals in contrast to Jewish thought and biblical support for God's providential care of all creatures.
- It presents a challenge to God's omnipotence because the purportedly perfect deathless paradise God created was too fragile to withstand the sins of Adam and Eve without being compromised.
- It presents a challenge to God's omniscience because God should have anticipated the sin of Adam and Eve and acted accordingly to prevent the Fall and the suffering it would cause.
- It is defeated by scientific evidence that shows death and pain existed in creation before the existence of Adam and Eve.

Therefore, while the Fall theodicy was once an influential means of understanding the problem of pain and death in the created order, it is no longer a robust explanation for creaturely suffering.

2.5 Other Corruption of Creation Theodicies

Scientific evidence showing death and pain preceded the existence of Adam and Eve has been a powerful defeater for the argument that God's perfect creation was corrupted by fallen humans. In response, some scholars have turned to other corruption of creation approaches that suggest suffering is the work of shadowy dark, chaotic, or demonic-like forces.

2.5.1 Dark Powers and Shadow-Sophia Corruption Theodicies

Nicola Hoggard Creegan uses Jesus' parable of the Wheat and the Tares (Matt 13:24–30, 36–43) to blame "dark powers" for causing harms in the ecosphere (2013: 82–96, 127–137). Regarding this parable, in which an enemy sowed weeds among a field of newly planted wheat, Jesus explicitly stated (Matt 13:37–39 NRSV): "The one who sows the good seed is the Son of Man; the field is the world, and the good seed are the children of the kingdom; the weeds are the children of the evil one, and the enemy who sowed them is the devil; the harvest is the end of the age, and the reapers are angels." Yet, Creegan never explicitly identifies the dark powers of her theodicy with either the devil, Satan, or demonic forces, making it more difficult for the reader to evaluate who or what she is empowering with culpability (87).

While Creegan's dark powers approach circumvents the problem of suffering before the existence of human beings, it does not explain how or when creation's dysfunction began. Did God create the dark powers, or did they coexist with God from the beginning as in dualistic Zoroastrianism or

Manicheanism, where good and evil are locked in a cosmic battle for existence? Creegan offers no clear answer as she denies accusations of dualism while admitting a provisional Christian dualism is warranted by her proposal (127). Furthermore, she admits she extends this parable beyond its original scope to present a negative force in the world with sufficient power to undermine God's plans for creation: a view not supported elsewhere in Scripture (91).

Celia Deane-Drummond offers another corruption of creation approach but rejects Satan, whom she views as a mythological figure, as a possible causal agent (2009: 187). Instead, she suggests a *shadow-sophia* in opposition to God caused "the dark possibility of evil in the world" after the Fall of humanity (2008: 20–21; 2009: 186). To avoid claims of dualism, she asserts shadow-sophia is not an ontological force of reality, but a "privation of the good, a state of creaturely being, or rather nonbeing" (2008: 21). However, if the Fall interpretation is no longer tenable, then how could a shadow-sophia come into existence after the human Fall? Moreover, how is it possible for the shadow-sophia to have agency and act upon the created order? Without ontological existence, how does privation of the good or nonbeing explain earthquakes, forest fires, or viruses? Since Deane-Drummond leaves the connection between the shadow-sophia and empirically observable examples of natural evil ambiguous, this corruption of creation theodicy remains weak.

2.5.2 Primordial Chaos Corruption Theodicies

Others appeal to primordial chaos as an alternative source of corruption in God's good creation. This is likely due to the lingering influence of Hermann Gunkel, who promoted *Chaoskampf* theory, claiming *təhôm* (the deep; sea) from Gen 1:2 reveals a mythological struggle between the Creator God and a primeval chaos represented by the waters of the deep and the Babylonian goddess Tiamat (1997:126–132; 2006).

While this theory was readily embraced by some academics, more recent scholarship has significantly undermined Gunkel's claims. *Təhôm* is unlikely to have been derived from *ti'âmat* since evidence suggests *təhôm* and *ti'âmat* originated separately from the proto-Semitic root *tiham* (Westermann 1994: 104–106; Johnston 2002: 119–120; Tsumura 2005: 36–76; Sollereder 2019: 20). Rather than referring to a pagan goddess, this "proto-Semitic" word *tiham* may originate from Sumerian (ti-ḫa$_2$-a-am$_3$) and hold positive connotations, translating as something like "to be waters of diverse and plentiful life" (Halloran 2006: 277, 109, 1, 18). The Apostle Peter also portrayed the *təhôm* positively: "Long ago by God's word the heavens existed and the earth was formed out of water and by water" (2 Pet 3:5b NIV) – a benevolent character-ization of the waters of the deep in the creation event. It is therefore unwarranted for scholars to suggest predation, pain, parasitism, disease, or death have been caused by a primordial chaos standing in opposition to God.

2.5.3 Prehuman Angelic Fall, Satanic, and Demonic Corruption Theodicies

It has been more commonly suggested predation, pain, disease, and death are the result of a prehuman angelic fall that perverted God's good creation (Trethowan 1954: 128; Mascall 1956: 301–302; Lloyd 1998; Boyd 2001: 293–318; Lewis 2001: 137–140). In this view, Satan, demons, or other evil spirits are responsible for harms and death in the created order.

Compared to the previous approaches, Satanic/demonic corruption of cre-ation theodicies have the strongest support. First, numerous biblical texts affirm the existence of Satan, the devil, and demons (Job 1:6–7; Matt 4:1–11; 13:37–42; Luke 10:18). Not only did Jesus accuse some of worshipping the devil in his own day (John 8:44), but there are extrabiblical accounts of people who have worshipped Satan both in the past, as described by King James I in *Demonology* (2008 [1597]), as well as the present in the Church of Satan – the first above-ground church dedicated to the devil and established in San Francisco, California, in 1966 (Church of Satan website). Consequently, there are biblical and historical reasons to support the existence of Satan and demonic entities.

Second, the Bible supports the claim that Satan and demons are allowed to afflict human beings with harmful tribulations. In the book of Job, Satan has the power to:

- Entice the Sabeans and Chaldeans to kill Job's servants and steal his livestock (Job 1:13–15, 17).
- Call down fire from heaven to kill livestock and people (Job 1:16).
- Summon a strong wind to collapse the house sheltering Job's adult children who were subsequently killed (Job 1:18–19).
- Afflict Job with painful sores from the soles of his feet to the top of his head (Job 2:7).

Scripture claims demons can also cause suffering:

- An evil spirit tormented King Saul after he broke relationship with God (1 Sam 16:14).
- A demon afflicted a child, causing him to convulse and throw himself into the fire (Luke 9:38–43).
- A legion of demons possessed and tormented a man on the shore of Gerasenes (Mark 5:1–20).

- Jesus sent out the twelve Apostles to drive out demons and to cure diseases (Luke 9:1).

However, problems arise when scholars suggest Satan and his minions have the power and authority to cause the predation, pain, parasitism, disease, and death associated with natural evil in *violation* of God's will.

First, although Satan may gain permission to inflict harm, he may not do so more than God permits (Job 1:8–12; 2:1–6). Second, biblical accounts imply Satan's power is neither limitless nor arbitrary, but intentionally directed toward the purpose of testing, tempting, and taking human souls (Luke 22:31–32; 1 Pet 5:8). Thus, the biblical record suggests the devil's power is permitted by God in order to test human souls, not to make animals eat each other for the sake of marring creation.

Two additional problems arise from blaming a purportedly corrupt creation on an angelic fall. First, the notion that fallen angels were responsible for perverting the natural order originated from Greco-Roman philosophical influences in the early church. Influential Christian thinkers like Tertullian, Athenagoras, and Origen "argued that famines, scorching winds and pestilence were not 'natural' in God's creation" and were instead the actions of spirits rebelling against God (Boyd 2001: 294–295). However, Scripture refutes this depiction of reality with God sending scorching winds (Jonah 4:8), punishing with earthquake, whirlwind, tempest, and consuming fire (Isa 29:6), and directing famine and pestilence against God's enemies (Jer 24:10). So, it was a misrepresentation by early church theologians to suggest God has nothing to do with either the ecological systems or hardships found in the created order.

The second problem with the angelic fall narrative arises from scholars' use of gap theory to support a prehuman fall of creation. The *Scofield Reference Bible* (1907) helped popularize the belief that "the cosmic fall is implicit in the biblical record from Genesis 3 to Revelation 22" (Bruce 1963: 169; Bimson 2006: 66–67). However, John Bimson points out that "a pre-human fall of the non-human creation is referred to nowhere in the Bible," and "can only be shoehorned into Genesis 1:1–2 by strained exegesis that goes against the grain of Hebrew grammar and syntax." Neither the sentence structure nor the Hebrew verb tenses support gap theory, which "draws no support from the text, but rather brings its own framework, digging its own imaginary gap between the two verses in order to set it up" (Blocher 1984: 41–43; Hamilton 1990: 115–116). In other words, the claim of a prehuman angelic fall occurring between the first two verses of Genesis 1 is an argument from silence, not substance. Consequently, the biblical text offers little to suggest Satan or demonic forces corrupted the good creation God made.

In summary, corruption of creation theodicies attempt to weaken the argument behind Rowe's theological premise (2) by deflecting responsibility for creaturely suffering and death away from God and placing blame upon malevolent powers in opposition to God instead.

The strengths of *corruption of creation theodicies* are:

- They have the advantages of the Adamic Fall theodicy without being vulnerable to scientific evidence that shows death and pain existed in creation before the existence of Adam and Eve.
- They offer a theological explanation for pain and death experienced by humans and nonhumans in the created order.
- There is biblical support for the existence of Satan, the devil, and demonic entities.
- The angelic fall has been an acceptable theological worldview among Western Christians and scholars from at least the time of Tertullian (ca. 155 CE).

The weaknesses of these theodicies are:

- They present a challenge to God's omniscience because God should have foreknown the threat from the shadowy dark, chaotic, or demonic forces and acted accordingly to prevent them from corrupting creation's goodness.
- They present a challenge to God's omnipotence because the purportedly perfect deathless paradise God created was too fragile to withstand the attacks of malevolent forces without being compromised.
- They depict a God who, if omnipotent and omniscient, is indifferent to protecting humans and nonhumans from suffering inflicted by malevolent forces.
- The angelic fall theodicies appear to be heavily dependent upon a Greco-Roman hermeneutical worldview rather than the Jewish and ANE milieu of the Old Testament texts.
- The claim shadowy dark, chaotic, or demonic forces have the power to violate and overwhelm the power and will of God has little to no support in the biblical text.
- There is no scientific evidence to suggest the biological world has ever been free of predation, ecological cataclysms, or death.

Therefore, while corruption of creation theodicies appear to be attractive alternatives to the Adamic Fall theodicy, they often have little empirical or biblical support even as they undermine classical doctrines of God's omnipotence and omniscience. These approaches suggesting shadowy dark, chaotic, or demonic-like forces thwarted God's will and destroyed God's intended paradise imply God's creations have more power over God's plans than God does, a contention that is neither supported by Scripture nor sufficiently explains creaturely suffering (Ps 33:10–11; Jer 10:10–11; Isa 55:10–11).

2.6 Animal Afterlife and Saint-Making Theodicies

A growing number of theologians acknowledge that the existence of animal pain is credible, animals are theologically significant to God, and corruption of creation arguments are unable to explain why animal suffering exists. Therefore, to reduce the strength of Rowe's theological premise (2), some theologians begin with a natural order–like defense then suggest God allows animals to suffer in this life because they will be healed and blessed in the afterlife. These approaches acknowledge God's omnipotence and omniscience and accept God's responsibility for creaturely suffering and death but argue the eternal bliss creatures experience after death will compensate any negative experiences in life (McDaniel 1989: 44–47; Southgate 2008: 78–91; Murray 2011: 41–72; Dougherty 2014: 134–178; Sollereder 2019: 156–182; Schneider 2020: 219–269).

Influential leaders and scholars in the church have long advocated for the theological dignity of animals. Theologians like St. Basil the Great of the Eastern Orthodox Church, St. Francis of Assisi of the Roman Catholic Church, and more modern thinkers like John Polkinghorne of the Anglican Church contend all creatures matter to God (Ugolino 1998: Chapter 16; Polkinghorne 2004: 147; Dougherty 2014: 158–159). The Armenian liturgy proclaims all creatures "will be renewed at the resurrection, that day which is the last day of earthly existence and the beginning of our heavenly life" (Dougherty 2014: 159). John Wesley, founder of the Methodist movement, also preached God's complete restoration of animals in the new creation (1872).

Christopher Southgate agrees animal afterlife can compensate creatures whose lives were either too short or disadvantageous for them to achieve their full potential and distinguishes various levels of creaturely flourishing (2008: 64, 84–85):

- **Fulfilled:** a state in which the creature is utterly being itself, in an environment in which it flourishes (including an appropriate network of relationships with other organisms), with access to the appropriate energy sources and reproductive opportunities.
- **Growing toward fulfillment:** not yet mature, but still with the possibility of attaining the "fulfilled" state.

- **Frustrated:** held back in some way from fulfillment, whether by adverse mutation or environmental change, or through old age, or being predated upon or parasitized, or being unable to find a mate through competition or species scarcity.

While Southgate's categories help explain why animal suffering must be overcome in the afterlife (78–91), there is a danger of viewing creaturely success and failure purely along biological metrics. Like Draper, some scholars tend to assume human and nonhuman creatures cannot flourish or experience completeness without perfect health, long life, and reproductive fruitfulness. Such perspectives overlook how social acceptance and affectionate relationships can enhance and transform creaturely experience, enabling a sense of flourishing even in the midst of tribulations. Flourishing can be observed in human lives despite the presence of deafness, blindness, injury, childlessness, or poverty, so why might not the same be true for animals? Therefore, theologians should hesitate to assume creaturely fulfillment can be solely based upon categories of biological "success." Nevertheless, animal afterlife theodicies provide robust compensation for creaturely suffering, find some degree of support in Scripture (Isa 11:6–9; Rom 8:19–22), and can be theologically plausible by postulating everything God declared "good" in the old creation (Genesis 1) would be present in the new creation (Revelation 21–22), including nonhuman animals.

While agreeing afterlife compensates animals for their suffering, Dougherty suggests the reason *why* God allows animals to suffer is to enable them to become saints (2014: 134–153). He contends animals bear the image of God and God will gift animals posthumously with the cognitive ability to be deified, make meaning of their suffering, and experience joy by accepting their pain and martyrdom as part of God's plan (143–148). However, each creature's peace in heaven is conditional upon reconciling with God and being virtuous, echoing a perspective that claims animals and nature are either fallen or sinful and must exhibit appropriate mentalities and/or behaviors for redemption and afterlife in heaven (153; Deane-Drummond 2008: 20–24; Moritz 2014: 362–374). John Schneider agrees animals can become saints, experiencing martyrdom on earth through suffering. Moreover, since cats and dogs love praise, Schneider suggests animals will receive praise, admiration, and gratitude from God and the angelic host for their painful sacrifices (2020: 261–269).

These saint-making theodicies of Dougherty and Schneider make admirable attempts to offer additional afterlife compensation but appear to be ad hoc explanations for animal suffering. First, they anthropomorphize animals too much, as though animals were inadequately created in Genesis 1 and can only be compensated by becoming cognitively and morally more humanlike in the new creation. Second, the notion suffering animals must earn their place in heaven through self-reflection or virtuous behavior seems to add insult to injury by suggesting animals must work to earn God's favor and consolation. Theologians who claim creatures are sinful or lack heaven-worthy virtues implicitly assume animals have a deficient relationship with God, making them unfit for heaven. Yet, animals do not break relationship with their Creator by mistaking themselves for God as humans do and Scripture suggests animals are always embraced by the love and providential care of God (Job 38–39; Matt 10:29; Birnbaum 1975: 172–173).

Third, proponents of animal saint-making theodicies offer no scriptural support for either the sinfulness, deification, moral agency, sainthood, or martyrdom of animals. Moreover, Dougherty and Schneider stretch concepts of martyrdom and sainthood beyond recognition. "Martyr" comes from the Greek *martus* meaning "witness" and was used to describe Apostles and Christians who suffered or died to bear witness to the life and resurrection of Jesus Christ (Oden 1992: 582). So how can animals who died from predation or disease be plausibly associated with people who died to pass on the Christian faith? Moreover, the word "saint" comes from *sanctus* (Latin) meaning "holy or consecrated" (Oden 1992: 660). The Greek (*hagios*) and Hebrew (*qadosh*) words for sacred/holy are only connected in Scripture to God, the things of God, angels, and human beings ... never animals. Therefore, no matter how well intended, applying "sainthood" to animal suffering bears little resemblance to the traditional usage of the term in the Christian faith.

In summary, *animal afterlife* and *saint-making theodicies* have the following strengths:

- They acknowledge the existence of animal pain is credible and animals are theologically significant to God.
- They acknowledge God's omnipotence, omniscience, and responsibility for suffering in the created order.
- They offer restoration and compensation in the blissful afterlife for suffering experienced by nonhumans in the created order.
- Animal afterlife theodicies have some level of church tradition and scriptural support for animal resurrection and immortality in the new creation.

The weaknesses of these theodicies are:

- Theologians can often emphasize either biological or anthropocentric priorities over theocentric values that are directed toward God's love-oriented care for individual creatures.

- Animal saint-making theodicies claim without scriptural support that animals who have suffered must work to earn God's favor and consolation.
- Animal saint-making theodicies claim without scriptural support that animals can be moral agents, saints, and martyrs and try to justify animal suffering by using the terms "saint" and "martyr" in ways that bear little resemblance to their traditional usage in the Christian faith.
- Animal saint-making theodicies offer a theologically speculative addendum to more scripturally plausible animal afterlife theodicies.

2.7 Seeking a New Theodicy for Suffering

The preceding analysis describes strengths and weaknesses of approaches offered to address the evidential problem of natural evil. The strongest approaches appear to be *natural order defenses, kenosis approaches,* and *animal afterlife theodicies.* If combined, these begin to offer a robust explanation for creaturely suffering that:

- Acknowledges the existence of animal pain is credible and animals are theologically significant to God.
- Acknowledges God's omnipotence, omniscience, and responsibility for suffering in the created order.
- Appeals to natural laws widely accepted in science.
- Emphasizes the empirically observable benefits of order and regularity in the cosmos.
- Notes the advantages of dynamic over static ecosystems.
- Lessens notions of wastefulness in nature.
- Points to empirically observable life/death/life cycles found in nature.
- Recognizes death of one creature creates opportunity for life of another.
- Recognizes the same neurocognitive ability to perceive pain enables a creature to perceive pleasure.
- Depicts a God who cares for and is near to all creatures that suffer.
- Offers a scripturally sound narrative of restoration and compensation in the afterlife for the suffering experienced by humans and nonhumans.

Nevertheless, a combined *natural order, kenosis, animal afterlife theodicy* would still lack:

- A depiction of God mitigating creaturely suffering in this life.

However, since this can be addressed by understanding suffering more deeply, this work will (1) engage the scientific literature to analyze neurocognitive aspects of pain perception along the evolutionary spectrum, (2) consider necessary features of ecological balance in healthy ecosystems, and (3) ascertain whether naturally occurring pain mitigation processes exist in nature. This approach will test claims regarding natural evil and offer a *theodicy of God's providential care* that:

- Affirms the existence of animal pain.
- Affirms God's concern for animals.
- Affirms God's omnipotence and omniscience.
- Affirms God's responsibility for the existence of pain.
- Affirms God's loving care of creatures.
- Affirms God's existence.

Theists need to appreciate the concerns of those who think theistic Judeo-Christian belief is compellingly undermined by scientific evidence. Therefore, in order to test the strength of atheists' arguments on their own terms, the scientific method will be considered the "gold-standard" for investigating the natural order and neo-Darwinian evolutionary theory will be assumed, employing both Darwin's theory of evolution by natural selection and Gregor Mendel's theory of genetics.

Usually, philosophers and theologians focus solely on Darwinian natural selection since it is most closely associated with the death of creatures or the inability of an organism to successfully pass on heritable traits. However, it hinders the analysis of suffering to ignore beneficial versus detrimental genetic factors when determining whether a stronger or weaker evolutionary impetus exists for the selection of pain in a creature. This becomes relevant when comparing evolutionary pressures for and against pain perception in invertebrates and vertebrates (Section 3.4).

Nevertheless, the theological perspective of this work is grounded in *theistic evolution* – the position that belief in an all-powerful, all-good God is compatible with the theory of evolution. This position takes the view that as God spoke creation into existence, God brought the natural laws that order the cosmos into being, where the laws of physics empower the laws of chemistry, which subsequently define the laws of biology. Through these structures of cosmic order, God created a universe in which living organisms could arise and natural ecosystems could unfold. Therefore, while neo-Darwinian evolutionary theory is currently the best explanation for the mechanisms that brought living biodiversity into existence, theistic evolution acknowledges God as the originator of those mechanisms.

3 Pain Perception across Species

Many arguments against the existence of a loving God involve empirical claims of widespread gratuitous pain among most creatures in the natural world for millions of years. However, the plausibility of such claims must be evaluated in order to assess their force in the argument from natural evil. Routinely, such sweeping claims are cited as evidence God is either cruel or indifferent or more probably there is no God and the universe is purely apathetic toward suffering. In other words, the evidence is better explained by atheism than theism. Both scientists and philosophers have cited pain in the natural world as the primary atheistic evidence. For example, Oxford ethologist and evolutionary biologist Richard Dawkins presents the cruel picture of nature atheists depend upon to construct their arguments of natural evil against theism (2008: 131–132):

> If Nature were kind, she would at least make the minor concession of anesthetizing caterpillars before they are eaten alive from within. But Nature is neither kind nor unkind. She is neither against suffering nor for it. Nature is not interested one way or the other in suffering, unless it effects the survival of DNA. It is easy to imagine a gene that, say, tranquilizes gazelles when they are about to suffer a killing bite. Would such a gene be favored by natural selection? Not unless the act of tranquilizing a gazelle improved that gene's chances of being propagated into future generations. It is hard to see why this should be so, and we may therefore guess that gazelles suffer horrible pain and fear when they are pursued to the death – as most of them eventually are. The total amount of suffering per year in the natural world is beyond all decent contemplation. During the minute it takes me to compose this sentence, thousands of animals are being eaten alive; others are running for their lives, whimpering with fear; others are being slowly devoured from within by rasping parasites; thousands of all kinds are dying of starvation, thirst and disease. It must be so. If there is ever a time of plenty, this very fact will automatically lead to an increase in population until the natural state of starvation and misery is restored.

Claims of creation's indifference toward suffering are presented by philosophers like Philip Kitcher as well (2013: 176):

> I do think that the Darwinian account of the history of life intensifies the troubles that Christianity faces in addressing the problem of evil. . . . For at least two hundred million years there have been animals capable of feeling pain, and that most of these have had lives that were dominated by pain. Nor is the pain accidental to the dynamic process, presumably instituted by a benevolent creator, for the evolution of life. The struggle for existence shows up in such "benign" strategies as those of the ichneumonidae (wasps) that paralyze the motor nerves of the caterpillars in which they lay their eggs – sensory nerves are intact as the young eat their way out. Darwin cited this as

a prime example of the difficulties that attend the view that species were separately created by a wise and benevolent being, but it is no less challenging if the mode of creation is indirect: why would any such being introduce a lengthy life-history in which this sort of strategy is written into the basic script?

Because claims regarding animal suffering are the backbone of the argument from natural evil, the theist should critically examine the validity of these claims. If the claims are true, they would appear to vindicate the atheist, but if they are false or misrepresentations of the world, then that realization would likely support the worldview of the theist.

3.1 Empirical Claims Regarding God's Cruelty in Nature

The following claims can be derived either explicitly or implicitly from Dawkins' and Kitcher's preceding statements:

1. Starvation and misery represent the normal state of creatures in nature.
2. Sufferings can be treated as objective quantifiable units that are cumulative.
3. It is doubtful a benevolent, loving, omnipotent God would need to create pain.
4. Most creatures are capable of suffering, from caterpillars to human beings.
5. The majority of animal lives are dominated by pain.
6. Animals endure unnecessary suffering from parasites, disease, and predators.

In light of these claims, it is appropriate to ask the following questions:

1. Is it accurate to depict starvation and misery as the "norms" in the natural world?
2. Is it appropriate to treat suffering as an objective quantitative entity?
3. Is pain biologically necessary and what happens to creatures when they cannot feel it?
4. Is it true most living creatures produced by evolutionary processes are capable of suffering?
5. Is it correct to claim most animals live in a perpetual state of pain most of their lives?
6. Does the evidence support the claim creatures endure unnecessary suffering from parasites, disease, and predator attack?

In addition to these claims, other examples have been cited contending the natural world is filled with unnecessary suffering and cruelty. A famous example is William Rowe's burned fawn suffering needlessly after being trapped during a forest fire (1979: 337). Other examples include Holmes Rolston's insurance chick that is killed through avian siblicide as well as killer whales who purportedly play with their prey before they eat them (1987: 137–140; 2003: 67). These are the pieces of evidence presented to claim the world was not created by the loving, benevolent, omniscient, omnipotent God of the Judeo-Christian faith, so it will be these claims that will be examined.

3.2 Mistaken Reasoning and Understandings of Pain

Well-meaning scientists and philosophers may accurately describe empirical observations of animal behavior in their arguments, but it may be asked whether they are sufficiently apprised of the scientific literature to understand the broader scope of what occurs in nature, especially regarding the problem of pain. This has caused misunderstandings regarding animal suffering, such as to what degree the neurocognitive capacity to perceive pain exists along the evolutionary spectrum (Section 3.3), and misconceptions related to natural processes and animal behavior (Section 4).

However, in other cases, proponents of atheistic metaphysical naturalism appear to make category errors or present distorted accounts of nature to further their arguments. Some examples will be addressed here.

3.2.1 Perpetual Starvation Versus Nature's Movement Toward Equilibrium

Dawkins asserts "if there is ever a time of plenty, this very fact will automatically lead to an increase in population *until the natural state of starvation and misery is restored.*" Since Dawkins does not appear to be contrasting a natural state versus an artificial state of starvation and misery, one must conclude he is claiming starvation and misery are the "normal" state of creatures in nature. However, this is a highly dubious claim since natural systems tend to move toward equilibrium where populations match food supply. Yet, Dawkins suggests nature perpetually moves toward a disequilibrium state, where starvation is the norm. This is not supported by empirical evidence, nor does Dawkins supply peer-reviewed scientific research to bolster his assertion. Whether famished animals are left to starve in misery will be addressed in Section 4.2.

3.2.2 The Subjective Nature of Pain

Pain is always subjective. This is the conclusion of the International Association for the Study of Pain (2011). Suffering is a subjective experience that is qualitative in nature, not a quantitative entity. Consequently, it is not an object to be summed over time or from creature to creature. Instead, each creature's pain must be addressed on an individual rather than a collective basis. This means "the total amount of suffering per year" cannot be quantified over time and species any more than animal play and satiation can be quantified over the ages. It is a meaningless statement because it makes the category error of treating a subjective value as an objective one.

Yet, this is what philosophers do when they argue that once all the pain and suffering over the ages is added together, one can safely conclude God does not love his creatures. That is a bit like suggesting if we add up all the crying of babies during human existence, we can safely conclude their mothers do not love them. It ignores the fact that suffering, which is a personal subjective experience, must be understood and comforted on a case-by-case basis. Each child that cries is comforted individually by the attending presence of its mother. It would be the product of unsound reasoning to suggest the cumulative sum of a baby's cries can prove the mother does not love it. By the same token, it is nonsensical to suggest a cumulative sum of creaturely pain is somehow evidence God does not love his creatures.

Instead of looking for abstract philosophical macro-solutions to the problem of creaturely suffering, it would be categorically sounder to understand suffering on the level of the individual creature's subjective experience. Therefore, a closer examination of pain experience leading to death will need to be considered before drawing conclusions about the compassionate nature of God.

3.2.3 Pain's Role in Survival and Healthy Longevity

Pain is a biologically necessary trait that enhances the odds of survival in more highly evolved creatures (Melzack and Dennis 1978: 1–26). Yet, Kitcher advocates for a reality where such creatures do not feel any pain, even when injured. However, such realities already exist and go by the names of *leprosy* and *congenital analgesia*, both being harmful conditions rather than beneficial to creatures. A creature that cannot perceive or respond to harmful stimuli cannot seek to protect itself from harm (Price and Dussor 2014: R384). The purpose of pain is to act as the body's warning system that physical damage is threatening its tissues.

An ordinary person who feels pain will limp when they have a blister on their foot, avoiding repetitive stress that would prevent healing. However, a person with *leprosy* who no longer feels pain will continue to walk on the blister until it becomes infected and repetitive stress causes bone fragments to break off and be discharged from the wound until there is no bone left (Brand and Yancey 1997: 123).

The inability to perceive the body's warning system, a condition called *congenital analgesia*, causes premature death in humans: "Children born with congenital insensitivity to pain are incapable of feeling pain and often die in the first few years of life because they injure themselves relentlessly, often falling victim to deadly infections" (Lieberman 2013: 44).

Pain is the body's protection mechanism. Increased sensitivity to pain near a wound is made possible by inflammation and a change in the local nerve cells, lowering their normal threshold for pain (Brand and Yancey 1997: 193; Butler and Finn 2009: 185). This ensures the body will quickly draw away from anything that comes in contact with the injured tissue, protecting the area from further damage.

While it may seem reasonable to assume creatures could have developed a warning system that would protect them from physical damage without causing pain, researchers like Dr. Paul Brand have discovered this is not the case. Gloves and socks with buzzers and flashing lights were designed for leprosy patients to warn when wearers were in danger of causing themselves physical harm, yet patients consistently ignored or overrode the systems. Patients disregarded these indirect warnings of pain, forcing researchers to realize artificial warning systems were useless unless they actually hurt (Brand and Yancey 1997: 193).

So, they designed a small battery-operated sensor that applied a harmless but painful electric shock to a part of the body that could still feel pain, like an armpit. Regrettably, it soon became clear their efforts were doomed as they observed one of the most conscientious volunteers discretely disconnecting the battery wire to avoid the warning shock as he struggled to loosen a rusted bolt (195–196). Other patients still participating in the study grew to resent the shocks, viewing them as punishment for "breaking the rules" rather than a protective artificial pain system. The researchers realized that while a healthy person recognizes internalized pain as a part of their own self-preservation mechanism, external signaling of pain would never be intimately linked with the person's sense of self (195):

> A person who never feels pain is task-oriented, whereas a person who has an intact pain system is self-oriented. The painless person may know by a signal that a certain action is harmful, but if he really wants to, he does it anyway. The pain-sensitive person, no matter how much he wants to do something, will stop for pain, because deep in his psyche he knows that preserving his own self is more significant than anything he might want to do.

Unfortunately, any warning system that does not cause sufficient pain to get the creature's attention and change their behavior will be ignored and ineffective.

Consequently, pain perception is the only way creatures will adequately protect themselves from tissue damage, enhancing their own chances for survival and healthy longevity (Price and Dussor 2014). In terms of natural selection, more intelligent long-lived species would be unlikely to exist without pain perception because they would be unable to respond appropriately to hazards found in their environment. In short, *pain is a necessary warning mechanism that contributes to the survival of more highly evolved creatures, helping to prevent their premature death, which would be an evil equally bad or worse than life with the possibility of pain.*

3.3 Nociception and Pain Along the Evolutionary Spectrum

When discussing animal pain, the philosophical community has tended to split between two extremes: the Cartesian/neo-Cartesian approach, which denies animals feel pain, and the anthropocentric approach, which contends most animals feel pain as humans do (Kuhse and Singer 1999: 640; Griffin 2004: 190–192). Yet, research from evolutionary biology and neuroscience shows these approaches fail to incorporate insights from evolutionary theory and animal neurophysiology; just as there is a diverse spectrum of evolutionary development across species, there is also wide variability among creatures to perceive pain. However, since the neo-Cartesian and anthropocentric understandings of animal pain both revolve around the human experience of pain, that is where this analysis will begin.

3.3.1 Components of Human Pain: Sensory and Distressing

When a person experiences physical injury, two different cortical regions of the brain are involved in the experience of pain, yet the two perceptions are experienced simultaneously as one: the *sensory* and *distressing* aspects of pain (Talbot et al. 1991; Rainville et al. 1997; Liberman 2013: 50–53).

Functional magnetic resonance imaging (fMRI) shows the *sensory aspects of pain* are detected in the *somatosensory cortex* and the *posterior insula* located in the parietal region (back half) of the brain. This region tracks the distinct areas of the body and distinguishes the variety and location of pain: a burn on the hand, a blister on the foot, a cut on the knee.

In contrast, the *distressing aspects of pain* are perceived in the medial frontal lobe of the brain in the *anterior cingulate cortex* (ACC), particularly the *dorsal anterior cingulate cortex* (dACC) and in the *anterior insula*. These regions in the top front center of the brain are responsible for producing the psychological distress associated with "suffering" (Casey and Tran 2006; Borsook et al. 2007).

Together, the sensory and distressing aspects of the human brain's response to harmful stimuli generate the phenomenon known as "pain":

$$PAIN_{(human)} = \text{Sensory Aspect (locational)} + \text{Distressing Aspect (emotional)}$$

Significantly, sensory experiences without accompanying emotional distress cannot be categorized as pain (Garland 2012). This is why an injured patient taking painkillers and no longer suffering is "no longer in pain." The injury remains, but their distressing emotional state is gone.

Consequently, a person or a species without a working ACC would be emotionally indifferent to the sensory aspects of a physical injury as demonstrated in *cingulotomy* patients whose ACCs were disconnected from surrounding brain regions. After the procedure, patients still felt the sensory aspects of noxious stimuli but no longer reported any associated distress (Foltz and White 1962: 89; Sharim and Pouratian 2016). Because cingulotomies eliminate the psychological distress normally associated with pain, creatures without the neurocognitive equivalent of an ACC would also be unlikely to experience any emotional distress from noxious stimuli.

Interestingly, the distressing aspect of pain appears to be uniquely associated with species capable of social relationships, namely mammals and birds, with birds having the neurocognitive equivalent of the ACC in the telencephalic region of their brains. In mammals, the ACC not only creates the psychological distress associated with *physical pain*, but the distress associated with *social pain* as well (Lieberman 2013: 39–70; Wager et al. 2013). In order to nurture social relationships and protect against social isolation, particularly between dependent mammalian young and their caregivers, nature uses the same ACC brain system to warn of damaged tissues and damaged relationships. In other words, the ACC activates whether the body detects a broken leg or a broken heart. This is due to a phenomenon known as the *brain opioid theory of social attachment*.

The connection between social relationships and the ACC begins with mother–infant social attachment behavior in mammals (Lieberman 2013: 47–50). The ACC has the highest density of opioid receptors in the mammalian brain and positive mother–infant interactions naturally release endogenous opioids, like endorphins. These bind to the ACC opioid receptors, providing feelings of contentment and relieving psychological distress. Consequently, separation of infants from their caregivers causes distressing opioid withdrawal-like pain for both the caregiver and infant, but once reunited their opioid levels increase back to normal and their emotional pain is relieved (Panksepp et al 1978).

This is significant because the *brain opioid theory of social attachment* shows non–life-threatening pain, whether caused by physical or social trauma, can be mitigated by the brain's naturally released painkillers. In other words, social animals like mammals and birds can comfort each other's pain through empathetic social interactions. While primates soothe by grooming one another, humans comfort each other with kind words (Dunbar 2003: 174; Inagaki and Eisenberger 2013). After a fight, ravens mitigate the distress of losers by offering beak-to-beak nudging and friendly preening (Waal 2013: 6). Distressed Asian elephants comfort one another with vocal communications and direct physical contact (Plotnik 2014). Chimpanzees console each other in times of distress with hugging and kissing (Waal 2013: 5). These behaviors employ *loving social interactions as a mechanism for pain mitigation and would be anticipated in a world created by a benevolent God whose value system is love.*

Notice, non-mammalian non-avian creatures lack the more highly evolved forebrain structures that generate the distressing aspect of pain. So, while other vertebrates (e.g., amphibians, reptiles) may perceive sensory aspects of an injury with their somatosensory cortex, they are unlikely to experience agony like mammals. Like cingulotomy patients, they would be aware of an injury without being distressed by it: detecting harm without suffering. This leads to a lower level of injury detection called *nociception.*

3.3.2 Nociception

According to *Recognition and Alleviation of Pain in Laboratory Animals*, it is important to distinguish between nociception and pain (USNAS 2009: 13–23; Garland 2012). *Noxious stimuli* are events that harm or threaten to harm tissues and activate special sensory nerve endings called *nociceptors* (Cervero and Merskey 1996; USNAS 2009: 13). While *nociception* represents the peripheral nervous system response to noxious stimuli, *pain* is the product of higher processing in the cerebral cortex (Section 3.3.1). Mammalian processing of noxious stimuli includes both the *nociceptive response* involving the spinal cord, brainstem, and thalamus and the *cognitive pain response* involving the cerebral cortex (USNAS 2009: 33–34; Fein 2014: 118–120).

Medical Surgical Nursing depicts this combined reaction to noxious stimuli in the example of burning one's hand on a stove. The text describes the nociceptive spinal reflex that causes a person to yank their hand away from the heat (White, Duncan, and Baumle 2013:112): "Cutaneous pain rapidly travels through a simple reflex arc from the nerve ending (point of pain) to the spinal cord at approximately 300 feet per second, with a reflex response evoking an almost immediate reaction. This is the reason when a hot stove is touched, the person's hand jerks back *before* there is conscious awareness of damage."

Observe that the quick motor response arises from the peripheral nervous system (in the hand) and the spinal cord alone. However, this is followed by an additional level of response involving the cerebral cortex:

> In the case of the hot stove, the sensory neuron also synapses with an afferent sensory neuron. The impulse travels up the spinal cord to the thalamus, where a synapse sends the impulse to the brain cortex. Once the impulse is interpreted, the information is consciously available. Then the person is aware of the location, intensity, and quality of pain. Previous experience adds the affective [emotional] feature to the pain experience.

Notice none of the nociceptive processes below the cerebral cortex cause the experience humans call pain. This has been verified by surgical preparations that sever the neural pathways below the cerebral cortex and show information generated by nociceptors below the level of transection cannot reach structures above the separation to trigger the cerebral cortex pain response (USNAS 2009: 33–34).

The US National Academy of Sciences provides examples where nociceptive responses to noxious stimuli can be observed without accompanying pain (2009: 19):

- In organisms with either no nervous system or a nervous system so simple scientists believe the organism is not capable of affect [emotion].
- In mammals whose forebrains are not receiving input from the periphery [after surgical transection].
- In humans whose pain has been suppressed [by analgesics/anesthetics].

For example, *automatic nociceptive responses* to noxious stimuli have been observed in situations where it has been clearly established the subject is *not* experiencing pain (19):

> In adult humans, postoperative cortisol output [an indicator of elevated stress response] is undiminished by analgesics that successfully treat the reported pain. . . . Sympathetic responses such as tachycardia [rapid heart rate], hypertension [high blood pressure], and pupil dilation occur in response to noxious stimuli in decerebrate rats and dogs [animals whose brainstem has been disconnected from the cerebral cortex].

Furthermore, *simple avoidance nociceptive responses* like withdrawal behaviors can be observed in subjects without a working cerebral cortex such as single-celled organisms as well as cats and rats whose neural connections to the brain have been severed. Other nociceptive responses observed despite the absence of pain include "turning of the head and neck toward the noxious stimulus, some vocalization, and the licking of affected paws" in decerebrate animals (19).

These experiments demonstrate that avoidance responses, reflexes, vocalizations, elevated blood pressure, rapid heart rate, and pupil dilation can be observed in creatures even when they are not feeling pain. Consequently, these cues are not definitive for correctly determining whether a creature may be experiencing pain. Therefore, in order to accurately evaluate the many sweeping claims about suffering in the world, it is important to differentiate creatures with only nociceptive neurological systems from creatures with the neurocognitive ability to perceive emotional distress associated with pain.

3.3.3 Distinguishing between Nociception and Pain in Animals

In order to distinguish creatures that experience pain from those merely exhibiting nociception, the US National Academy of Sciences determined creatures must (2009: 20):

1. Discriminate painful from nonpainful states.
2. Make decisions based on this discrimination in a way that cannot arise from nonconscious nociceptive responses.
3. Demonstrate motivations to avoid pain.
4. Display affective states of fear or anxiety if threatened with noxious stimuli.

They also note that animals experiencing pain might "exhibit spontaneous behavioral changes including sustained signals of distress and impairments in normal behaviors such as sleep" (20).

Such experiments have demonstrated mammalian and avian ability to discriminate between painful and nonpainful states. Rats with arthritis not only discern the difference between injections of aspirin and injections of saline, but even learn to select aspirin injections to reduce their pain. Research also demonstrates mammals and birds act to avoid pain or noxious stimuli, implying conscious awareness of pain (20):

• Rats, mice, primates, and pigeons lever-press to avoid electric shocks.
• Only rats and chickens with arthritis-induced lameness orally self-administer nonsteroidal anti-inflammatory drugs, not their healthy counterparts.

After much study, the US National Academy of Sciences has concluded the conscious experience of pain *is only strong for mammals and birds* (21). So, as neo-Cartesians argue no animals experience pain while anthropocentrists argue most animals feel pain, the Academy concludes the better assessment lies between these extremes (20–21). In other words, the empirical evidence only supports pain experience in more highly evolved animals: mammals and birds. Therefore, since evidence of pain is lacking for other taxa such as fish, reptiles, and amphibians, there is no scientific basis for philosophers to claim creatures other than mammals or birds can feel pain.

3.4 Claims Regarding Universal Creaturely Suffering

It is ironic atheists like Dawkins and Kitcher appeal to science to make their arguments, yet omit insights from pain-related science and neo-Darwinian evolutionary theory in their analysis of creaturely pain. They seem unaware that, according to the US National Academy of Sciences, empirical evidence only supports pain perception in the more highly evolved brains of mammals and birds. Moreover, Darwinian evolutionary theory would seem to make it rather obvious that less evolved organisms would lack the neurocognitive abilities of more evolved organisms. Consequently, while mammals have the capacity to experience the distressing and sensory aspects of pain to the degree their frontal and parietal lobes have evolved respectively, it would seem to be anthropocentric speculation to assume evolutionarily lower organisms perceive pain like mammals. In fact, many scientific studies confirm this is not the case.

The *Proceedings of the National Academy of Sciences* rejects claims that insects have subjective experience required for pain perception (Key, Arlinghaus, and Browman 2016). Moreover, entomologists observe that insects seem entirely oblivious to their injuries (Eisemann et al. 1984: 166):

> No example is known to us of an insect showing protective behavior towards injured body parts, such as limping after leg injury or declining to feed or mate because of general abdominal injuries. On the contrary, our experience has been that insects will continue with normal activities even after severe injury or removal of body parts. An insect walking with a crushed tarsus, for example, will continue applying it to the substrate with undiminished force. Among our other observations are those on a locust which continued to feed whilst itself being eaten by a mantis; aphids continuing to feed whilst being eaten by coccinellids; a tsetse fly which flew in to feed although half-dissected; caterpillars which continue to feed whilst tachinid larvae bore into them; many insects which go about their normal life whilst being eaten by large internal parasitoids; and male mantids which continue to mate as they are eaten by their partners. Insects show no immobilization equivalent to the mammalian reaction to painful body damage, nor have our preliminary observations of the response of locusts to bee stings revealed anything analogous to a mammalian response.

So, the scientific literature has noted the lack of pain response in insects for decades, yet proponents of metaphysical naturalism like Dawkins and Kitcher still try to bolster their arguments against the Judeo-Christian faith by citing the supposed pain of caterpillars caused by the ichneumonidae wasp whose larvae consume the caterpillar from within. But if insects do not have nervous systems with the equivalent of a frontal lobe to perceive pain, how can their existence be said to include the experience of suffering?

This counterintuitive concept of bodily destruction without pain might initially be difficult to accept, but during the last twenty-four hours the average adult human being endured the death of billions of their cells due to the process of apoptosis (programmed cellular death). Were all these people writhing in pain as their cells died? Obviously not, and the reason is because human bodies are not wired with a nervous system to detect this kind of death or destruction within the body. It would serve no purpose, so the human body did not evolve to experience pain due to apoptotic cellular death. In the same way, insects like the caterpillar did not evolve with the nervous system necessary to feel pain even when they are dying from within.

Neither caterpillars nor any other insect can feel pain. Yet Richard Dawkins declares, "If Nature were kind, she would at least make the minor concession of anesthetizing caterpillars before they are eaten alive from within" (2008: 131). Apparently, Nature has done just that since caterpillars cannot feel pain at all. So, perhaps it is time to realize Nature is far kinder than she is given credit for?

This inability to perceive the distress associated with "pain" is not unique to insects. It also appears to be lacking in the entire category of animals classified as invertebrates. According to the International Association for the Study of Pain, it is the subjective, emotional component that causes pain in a creature, not the activation of nociceptive receptors in the body (2011). So, while invertebrates have the capacity to experience a nociceptive response to noxious stimuli, they do not have the neurocognitive psychological capacity to suffer (Canada Senate Standing Committee on Legal and Constitutional Affairs [CSSCLCA] 2003a). This conclusion is based upon (1) the evolutionary function of pain, (2) the neural capacity of invertebrates, and (3) the observed behavior of invertebrates (CSSCLCA 2003b).

First, in the case of vertebrates, the perception of emotionally distressful pain is an evolutionary advantage as an educational tool to avoid harms that could affect the longevity of the animal (Melzack and Dennis 1978: 1–26). Because vertebrates are generally longer-lived than invertebrates, they have more time to learn from experiences of both pain and pleasure that in turn will improve their chances for survival. In contrast, invertebrate lifespans tend to be shorter and their behavior is largely thought to be genetically determined. Consequently, there is weaker evolutionary impetus for the selection of pain in invertebrates (Eisemann et al. 1984).

Second, the neural capacity of invertebrates, with the exception of cephalopods (e.g., octopus, squid), has been found to be quite limited compared to vertebrates (Matheson 2002). Invertebrate nervous systems are composed of many small brains (ganglia) with relatively few neurons distributed throughout their nervous systems. As such, they are thought to have limited cognitive capacity since they have evolved without the complex nervous system required for the development of a psychological response like suffering. Cephalopods have been considered a possible exception to this because of their larger centralized nervous systems, which share similarities to those of fish (Smith 1991). However, a recent review of the literature on pain perception in fish (evaluating more than 200 peer-reviewed scientific papers) has concluded that while fish demonstrate nociceptive responses to negative stimuli, they do not have the neurophysiological capacity to perceive pain or suffer in a conscious fashion as humans do (Rose et al. 2014). The neurobiologists, behavioral ecologists, and fishery scientists who examined the literature concluded most studies investigating fish ability to perceive pain were flawed. For example, researchers did not adequately consider the significant anatomical and neurophysiological differences between humans and fish that would suggest very different perception capabilities between the species (111–114). Also, methodologies failed to distinguish between unconscious nociceptive perception and conscious perception of emotional suffering, making it impossible to deduce emotional states from fish behavior (104–109). Consequently, human interpretations of fish responses too often simply assumed the presence of emotional pain. Furthermore, pain killers like morphine had no effect on fish, suggesting fish are either completely oblivious to pain in human terms or they respond to pain in a way unrecognizable to human observers. In fact, dosages given to fish at "10 times the lethal dose for any bird or mammal that has ever been studied" were insufficient to "alter the swimming behavior of the trout" (107). The reviewers concluded "fish responses to nociceptive stimuli are limited and fishes are unlikely to experience pain" (97). It is therefore logical to conclude that if vertebrates like fish lack the psychological ability to suffer, it is even less likely invertebrate cephalopods would have such capacity.

Third, there is little indication of emotion in invertebrates. Most invertebrates lack social behaviors, with many cannibalistically eating their own young. Social behavior is absent in cephalopods as well, who do not provide parental care for their young, suggesting their ability to hunt, hide from predators, and communicate must be genetically determined rather than learned behaviors (Hanlon and Messenger 1996). Furthermore, many invertebrates, like the insects cited earlier, continue to behave normally even after severe injury. Consequently, based upon the three criteria mentioned above, it is reasonable to conclude invertebrates have not evolved the neurocognitive ability to perceive emotional suffering.

This is significant because it provides empirically derived, scientifically based reasoning to exclude the vast majority of species on earth from the category of those that suffer. According to Oxford zoologist Robert May, approximately 2,507,500 animal species are invertebrates and the other 41,300 are vertebrates (1988: 1446). This means 98.4 percent of animal species on earth have evolved to live and die, but will never experience the emotional distress associated with suffering. The remaining 1.6 percent of earth's animal species that are vertebrates may or may not be able to experience suffering, but like fish, many of these species appear to lack the psychological capacity to perceive pain.

For example, researchers note the challenges of studying pain in reptiles. They observe captive reptiles frequently suffer thermal burns because they perch themselves too close to heat sources and do not move even when their tissue is being damaged (Mosley 2011: 49). Consequently, if some reptiles are so insensitive to harmful stimuli they do not move to protect themselves, it seems even less likely reptiles experience traumatic psychological anguish. Furthermore, reptilian anatomy lacks the neurophysiological structures needed to experience the distressing aspect of pain since "the ACC is one of the neural adaptations that distinguishes mammals from our reptilian ancestors" (MacLean 1985: 405; Lieberman 2013: 51).

It is also doubtful amphibians have the neurocognitive psychological capacity to perceive emotional suffering since they are even less evolved than reptiles, leaving birds (*Aves*) and mammals (*Mammalia*) as those most likely to experience emotional distress among species. With approximately 9,000 species of birds and 4,500 species of mammals, this means only about 13,500 species, or 0.5 percent of all species on earth, have the capacity to experience suffering (May 1998). So, when metaphysical atheists categorically lump all creatures together in one great heaping mass of misery, the science suggests they are making a claim that cannot be substantiated by the empirical evidence.

4 Natural Processes and Animal Behavior

Besides misleading assertions that most creatures endure lives of intense suffering and misery, metaphysical atheists also misrepresent the natural processes of earth's ecosystems as being unnecessarily cruel and inefficient. Examples of suffering are often either distortions of what occurs in nature or anthropocentric interpretations of animal behavior. Furthermore, death and destruction are often incorrectly conflated with suffering and cruelty: a questionable association at best. However, scientific findings can correct such distortions and aid in developing an improved response to the atheistic argument from natural evil. Therefore, the following sections will offer a more thorough understanding of natural processes found in ecosystems regarding forest fires, predation, parasitism, disease, famine, and claims of animal cruelty.

4.1 Forest Fires

In 1979, William Rowe created the infamous image of a burned fawn suffering a prolonged agonizing death to argue God allows unnecessary suffering (337):

> Suppose in some distant forest lightning strikes a dead tree, resulting in a forest fire. In the fire a fawn is trapped, horribly burned, and lies in terrible agony for several days before death relieves its suffering. So far as we can see, the fawn's intense suffering is pointless.

In reality, it may be more accurate to say Rowe's imagined scenario is pointless, or at least highly improbable. In contrast to the dire invention of philosopher Rowe, US Fish and Wildlife fire ecologist Bill Leenhouts reveals a completely different reality: "Don't worry about the animals. Most animals actually escape the fires" (James 2000). In fact, closer scrutiny of Rowe's caricature shows it has little in common with real-world animal behavior. As University of Idaho forestry specialist Yvonne Barkley clarifies (2019):

> Many people believe that all wildlife flees before the flames of a fire like the animated characters in the movie "Bambi." Contrary to this belief, scientists studying animal behavior during the 1988 burns in the Greater Yellowstone area saw no large animals fleeing the flames. Bison, elk, and other ungulates were observed grazing and resting, often 300 feet or less from burning trees.

These observations are among several reasons the suffering fawn scenario is so unlikely. Because most animals' sense of smell is excellent, wildlife is likely to smell smoke on the wind, providing ample time to move a safe distance from fire (Komarek 1969: 170). Furthermore, since wind driving the blaze sends smoke downwind into the direction the fire is traveling, it would seem a surprisingly accurate way of forewarning animals in its path. So rather than becoming trapped, the fawn would have sufficient time to move away from approaching fire to protected areas with other large wildlife.

This is not to say large animal mortality never occurs from wildfires, but when it does death is usually caused by smoke inhalation from large, fast-moving fires (Barkley 2019). In such cases, the animal is deprived of oxygen to the brain, quickly resulting in unconsciousness, then death. Consequently, these animals will not suffer if the flames reach their bodies. Unfortunately, it is often livestock restrained by fences that become "trapped" casualties of wild-fires (Brown 2012). Yet if cattle are unable to escape wildfires due to fences built by human hands, is their suffering effectively caused by God or human beings?

Those who suggest destructive processes in nature are evidence of God's cruelty or indifference often neglect fire's role as a natural and necessary part of healthy ecosystems, with plants and animals alike adapting to fire in the environment (Vogl 1973; Chang 1996). Highly mobile animals easily avoid heat and noxious gases by flying or moving away at the first scent of smoke. Low mobility animals like snails and other invertebrates have also adapted to fire-prone environments. Snails shelter their eggs and themselves in areas protected from fire. Even when larger numbers of snails and insects died after an intense fire (painlessly, since they are invertebrates), their populations returned to normal within a year (Komarek 1985: 5). Animals like the reed frog and red bat use chemo-reception of smoke, visual detection of flames/smoke, and sounds of fire to evade danger (Engstrom 2010: 116). Wrens and sparrows fly short distances away to shrub thickets near wet soil for protection. Lizards either burrow or climb trees to escape flames. Meadow voles flee to undisturbed areas or shelter underground. Multiple species of rattlesnakes were monitored sheltering safely in underground burrows during low intensity ground fires. Burrows generally provide safe shelters for younger, smaller, or less mobile animals where measured temperatures and CO_2 levels rise minimally in times of fire (Engstrom 2010: 117).

While primary fire effects cause little animal death, the more serious problem is destruction of habitat. Yet many plants and trees have not only adapted to fire, but require periodic fire for seed germination, the removal of dead vegetation, and the return of nutrients to the soil (Bonnet et al. 2005). Ponderosa pines in the Western United States survive fires because they have developed thick fire-resistant trunks and branches high out of reach from fires typically found in ecologically balanced forests (U.S. National Park Service 2017). Even though food and shelter are lacking immediately after fire, University of Idaho fire ecologist Leon Neuenschwander explains fires are actually necessary and advantageous for all wildlife: "In the long term, these wildfires will benefit all animals. In the short term, some animals will be displaced" (James 2000). The severity of this problem will be proportional to the size of the fire (Chang 1996: 1075). Smaller fires leave surviving habitats for forest animals to move into and meet their needs. While some creatures may move on, others move into the newly scorched area for the unusually nutrient-rich new plant growth that emerges from the ash debris. Burned areas of woodland return as meadowlands, providing an inviting environment for plants and animals that prefer open fields, organically rich soils, and additional sunlight. Such areas become lush with wildflowers, bees, and other pollenating insects along with the birds that feed on them. New meadows also attract deer, elk and mice as well as their predators: coyotes, bobcats, mountain lions, bears, and wolves (James 2000). It is the start of a refreshed cycle of the natural ecosystem that will become forest again with the passage of time.

Unfortunately, human interference has upset the natural ecology of forests in several ways, unnecessarily worsening the effects of fire for both plants and animals. First, human encroachment on forest lands reduces the overall acreage available to wildlife. This means less territory animals can migrate into when their habitat has been damaged by fire. Second, human fire suppression has unintentionally increased the severity and destructive power of wildfires when they do occur. Because fire suppression was the standard protocol for the past 100 years, the accumulation of dead wood and undergrowth has resulted in far more fuel for fires than would occur naturally, causing fires to burn hotter, higher, and longer than they would otherwise (U.S. National Park Service 2017). Fires of this magnitude can overwhelm species that would otherwise be suitably adapted to fire, like ponderosa pine (Lentile, Smith, and Shepperd 2005). While these overgrown fires may result in the unnecessary death of plants and animals, the responsibility would seem to lay at the feet of human beings, not the natural world.

Fires are a healthy part of forest ecosystems, being a necessary and beneficial balance of growth and destruction, life and death (Komarek 1969). As discussed previously, only mammals and birds are capable of experiencing the agony associated with pain. This means the creatures most vulnerable to fire are the ones *least* likely to feel pain, namely invertebrates and other non-mammalian, non-avian vertebrate species. In contrast, mammals and birds capable of feeling pain escape injury by fleeing or sheltering during fire. Creatures who die of asphyxiation lose consciousness and die very quickly due to lack of oxygen to their brains, consequently having little chance to perceive pain before their death. Accordingly, there is very little evidence to suggest animals suffer due to forest fires. Rather, animal behavior in nature minimizes pain resulting from such destructive events. It is therefore a distortion for scholars like Rowe to misrepresent complex, well-balanced natural systems as scenarios of natural evil and then accuse God of causing unnecessary suffering. On the contrary, the natural life and death processes of forest fires in healthy biomes have evolved in such a way as to minimize animal suffering while providing benefits for all the creatures therein. As such, these processes are consistent with a benevolent God who seeks to minimize suffering and creates new life even in the midst of death.

4.2 Pain, Predation, and Ecological Balance

In most philosophical discussions, predation is synonymous with natural evil and considered a primary source of suffering in nature. However, this assumption should be reconsidered in light of additional information on pain and animal behavior. To begin, it is important to distinguish the different types of pain available in more highly evolved creatures: acute, persistent, and chronic pain (USNAS 2009: 16).

Acute pain refers to momentary pain that quickly passes, like a pinch or needle prick, and warns the creature of immediate harm to tissues and causes rapid withdrawal from the danger. *Persistent pain*, like that of a sprained ankle, refers to pain that lasts for days or weeks as a creature heals and needs unpleasant sensory feedback to avoid further injury. *Chronic pain* is pain that continues past the time expected for healing and is typically associated with poorly healed injuries, age-related issues like arthritis and tissue degeneration, or destructive diseases like cancer. Unlike acute and persistent pain, chronic pain does not appear to produce survival benefits for the creature and seems to be an unhelpful side effect of the body's pain system, causing prolonged suffering. This is where the role of predators come in.

Predators detect prey animals that are injured, sick, or weak; in other words, they notice the animals most likely to be in pain or distress. Researchers observed black sea bass preferentially preyed upon injured squid over uninjured squid (Price and Dussor 2014: R384). The preference for distressed prey is probably an evolutionary development that minimizes the energy expenditure of the predator while maximizing their caloric intake (Butler and Finn 2009: 185). Moreover, predation minimizes the pain duration of weak or sickly animals that might otherwise suffer. This has been shown in scientific studies on predation.

For example, researchers wanted to determine whether predator birds killed randomly or by noticing specific features of individual prey. To test this, yellow-legged gulls were culled using two methods: predation by raptors, and shooting birds randomly. After veterinary analysis of the bird carcasses, researchers concluded predators did not kill at random, but preferentially selected their prey based upon age, muscle condition, and sickness. Birds with parasites, infections, diseased organs, injuries, or other weaknesses were statistically more likely to be killed by raptors than by random shooting, suggesting predators are better adapted to recognize distressed prey than human eyes (Genovart et al. 2010). Similar observations were made with mountain lions, which were four times more likely to kill deer sick with chronic wasting prion infections than their healthy counterparts, even when field observers had not detected noticeable illness before their deaths (Miller et al. 2008).

Predators detect the earliest changes in prey at the onset of debilitating conditions, suggesting prey are typically killed *before* they have to endure long-term pain. This conclusion, that predators are more likely to kill animals suffering from conditions that will result in chronic pain than their healthier counterparts, is also supported by related neurobiological evidence.

Stress-induced analgesia (SIA) is a natural part of the fight-or-flight response that suppresses pain while an animal is endangered by predators or other life-threatening situations (Basbaum and Fields 1984; Butler and Finn 2009). Analgesia (suppression of pain) is facilitated by the release of endogenous opioids and increases the animal's chances of survival by allowing it to focus on evading threats rather than tending to an otherwise painful injury (Reeder and Kramer 2005). Nevertheless, once danger has passed, nociception and pain perception become elevated, increasing pain sensitivity in tissues surrounding the injury to discourage normal behaviors that could inflict further damage (Basbaum et al. 2009; Price and Dussor 2014). SIA also helps mammals survive by minimizing signs of injury that attract predators.

However, SIA is reduced in animals with chronic pain where stressful events can actually trigger *hypersensitivity* to pain (Rivat et al. 2007; Butler and Finn 2009: 186). Reductions in SIA were also observed in animals subjected to other long-term stresses, like chronic malnourishment or REM sleep deprivation (Butler and Finn 2009: 188). These results suggest mammals weakened by naturally occurring long-term stresses, like famine or drought, may have diminished SIA, making it harder to hide painful body language from predators and resulting in the swift ending of the creature's suffering.

This may help explain predation behaviors known as "surplus killing," where predators kill more than they can immediately eat during times of extreme distress in a prey population. Besides killing suffering animals, predators help bring populations back into equilibrium with the environment's available resources and alleviate scarcity and suffering among remaining animals. Such behavior has been witnessed in crocodiles at watering holes in times of drought and wolves during extremely hard winters. So, if predatory behavior is driven not only by hunger but also by an instinctual motivation to kill suffering animals, it may explain why surplus killing occurs in times of distress. This predator–prey behavior was observed in Yellowstone National Park during the winter of 1996–1997 when inclement weather cut off grazing animals' food supply (Smith and Ferguson 2005: 129–130):

The heavy snow, then rain, then extreme cold turned the snowpack to concrete, sealing off grasses under a hard shell of ice – a catastrophic situation for ungulates. Before long both elk and bison began leaving the park in huge numbers, with thousands of elk dying along the way. . . . As for the wolves, in late winter of 1997 it seemed they couldn't kill enough elk. Indeed, this was the only year we've documented so-called surplus killing, which refers to wolves taking more than they can immediately eat. Even so, as we continued to watch those carcasses over the next few weeks, many of which did in fact still have meat on them, we saw wolves returning to feed a second and even a third time. . . . Despite a sordid mythology that paints wolves as bloodthirsty killing machines, in the vast majority of cases a wolf taking everything he can means just plain getting enough to keep going. For every hunt that leads to a kill a pack endures many times that number of failed attempts; in Yellowstone proper, only one out of every five attempts is successful.

First, this account supports the growing body of evidence that predators preferentially select suffering and distressed animals for their prey, limiting the pain these creatures would otherwise experience. Second, it suggests surplus killing only occurs when ecological factors stress an entire population of prey, as in times of famine or drought. Third, even though predators may kill more prey than they can immediately eat, other carnivores, scavengers, and decomposers will consume the carcass eventually. There is no waste in nature. Fourth, when predators are absent, prey animals must die slower, more protracted and painful deaths, either by starvation, parasitism, or disease. Fifth, not every predator attack will result in a kill as wildlife observation shows wolf predation is successful only 20 percent of the time.

Predator success rates are typically around 30 percent (Eysenck 2000: 173). Spotted hyenas inhabiting Kenya's Masai Mara National Reserve capture prey in approximately 33 percent of hunting attempts (Holekamp et al. 1997). Great white sharks, an apex predator, had a kill rate of about 48 percent during surface attacks on Cape fur seals near Seal Island (University of Miami 2018). While it might seem these sharks are better hunters, their higher kill rate is likely due to hunting solitary juveniles that are easy, inexperienced prey (Baird and Dill 1995: 1306, 1309). This is significant since philosophical contemplation of predation often assumes predators are guaranteed winners and treats them as unwelcome interlopers in an otherwise unspoiled natural system, yet this depiction of reality is inaccurate. In fact, mammalian predators that do not eat will suffer as much as their distressed prey. Furthermore, the entire ecosystem is weakened when predators are removed from the environment (Estes et al. 2011; Winnie and Creel 2017). The unintended consequences of predator absence can be seen most clearly in the case of Yellowstone National Park.

Without wolves in Yellowstone, elk lingered unhindered among young vegetation, grazing upon willow and cottonwood shoots growing along the park's waterways (Smith and Ferguson 2005: 15). This caused degradation of waterside environments, the loss of beaver populations, and an elk population that grew so large it had to be culled by human hunters lest the elk die of starvation. The reintroduction of wolves not only brought the elk population back into equilibrium but also initiated an unexpected trophic cascade that reached further into Yellowstone's ecosystem than researchers anticipated. Once the wolves' presence became reestablished, elk grazing behavior changed, causing them to avoid feeding along streams and rivers with low visibility. As a result, willows, cottonwoods, and other beleaguered vegetation reappeared and with their return came beavers. Renewed construction of beaver dams created additional ponds and waterways in the park that became home to populations of yellow and Wilson's warblers, muskrat, fish, waterfowl, and amphibians. Wolves also created safer habitats for prey animals like pronghorn deer, particularly pronghorn fawns experiencing predatory pressure from unchecked coyote populations (125).

Not only did the presence of these predators create and improve habitats for a greater diversity of species, but it also indirectly increased the food supply for many species. "In all the planning, all the studies," says biologist John Varley, "the one thing we totally underestimated was how many other mouths the wolves would feed" (Smith and Ferguson 2005: 121–122). Whenever wolves kill, there are scraps for scavengers. Biologists observed at least twelve different species of scavengers feeding off carcasses left by wolves, including ravens, magpies, and coyotes, as well as golden and bald eagles. The wolves also indirectly feed songbirds, like the mountain bluebird, which eat beetles and flies whose growth and development occur on carcass remains. Additionally, by decreasing the coyote population, wolves helped increase populations of other animals, like red foxes and rodents (Smith and Ferguson 2005: 125). Increased rodents meant an increase in food supply for owls and hawks, supporting their populations as well.

Studies show predators are not only necessary but also beneficial to other species, including prey animals. Without predators, animals suffer needlessly in times of starvation or when they become sick and weak. Predators have an instinct to kill animals showing signs of injury or distress. It must be emphasized that predation is a part of nature that, in fact, minimizes the suffering of creatures; it in itself is not the source of pain in nature. Medical ethicists argue quick deaths that shorten the experience of pain are often preferable to lingering deaths that prolong unnecessary suffering (Kuře 2011). As the *American Veterinary Medical Association Guidelines for the Euthanasia of Animals* states: "When animals are plagued by disease that produces insurmountable suffering, it can be argued that continuing to live is worse for the animal than death" (2020: 6). Human beings euthanize animals when they have painful conditions that are resistant to treatment: to allow protracted suffering rather than ending it is considered cruel (Rollin 2009). In the same way, animals with ailments that would eventually cause long-term pain and suffering are euthanized in nature by predators who seek out creatures that are sickly, weak, or in distress.

4.3 Perceptions of Predator-Targeted Animals

At this point, it is fair to pose the following query: "It may be true predators minimize pain and suffering in nature by euthanizing weak and sickly animals. It may also be true predators are a necessary part of balanced and healthy ecosystems. However, surely the pain an animal feels when it is being killed by predators is unnecessary and cruel?" Dawkins' commentary alleging Nature's indifference to suffering suggested Nature would be kinder if there was "a gene that, say, tranquilizes gazelles when they are about to suffer a killing bite" as we "guess that gazelles suffer horrible pain and fear when they are pursued to the death" (2008: 131). There are two requests here. First, a wish that animals would not experience pain and fear when pursued by predators, and second, a "tranquilizing effect" of some sort to calm prey before receiving the kill bite. It is therefore ironic Dawkins insists these accommodations would be evidence in favor of Nature's kindness (and indirectly theism) because that is unwittingly close to what Nature *has* provided.

Dawkins "guesses" gazelles suffer horrible pain and fear when they are pursued by predators, but the physiological evidence does not support this supposition. As mentioned previously, it is precisely the onset of stress or fear that induces SIA in mammals (Basbaum and Fields 1984; Butler and Finn 2009). Although fear may be an unwelcome emotion, that appears to be part of the point: it removes all other distractions from the creature's attention (Reeder and Kramer 2005: 226). Moreover, a major part of what makes feelings of fear so unpleasant is the corresponding cascade of stress hormones that prepare the creature's body for survival (Reeder and Kramer 2005: 225–228; Koenig 2007: 423–424). Cortisol inhibits insulin production and prepares the body to fight or flee by flooding it with glucose as an immediate energy source for muscles (Febbraio et al. 1998: 466–467; Aronson 2009: 38; University of Utah 2010). As cortisol constricts arteries, epinephrine increases the heart rate and together these cause the blood to pump harder and faster. In addition, epinephrine improves cognitive brain function, increasing awareness and alertness (Reece et al. 2011: 528). Endogenous opioids suppress pain perception in the animal, allowing the creature to focus on escaping from danger (Rivat et al. 2007). Other physiological changes like inhibition of digestion (associated with a queasy stomach) and shaking are partially due to the diversion of blood flow to large skeletal muscles needed for fighting and escape (Gleitman et al. 2010: 473–477). Another unpleasant but necessary side effect of the adrenal response is increased muscle tension throughout the body, providing the animal with additional strength and speed. But no matter how odious, none of these physiological changes or their corresponding emotional responses associated with fear are gratuitous or "painful." Rather, all are necessary to help the creature stay alive.

For most of us, it is hard to understand what it feels like to be prey in the presence of a predator. Most of our knowledge about predator attacks comes from watching nature documentaries, like Blue Planet or National Geographic, where the prey response can only be witnessed from a third-person point of view. As such, it is easy to impose our own notions of fear and pain upon the creatures viewed on television. However, unlike the animals being filmed, human beings sitting safely in a room would not only feel pain like a pinch or a cut to its full extent, but their ability to feel empathy also causes them to feel sympathetic pain in their own bodies as they watch animals being attacked (Lieberman 2013: 155). Therefore, observers must recognize their own bodies are in a completely different physiological state than the animals being observed. The animals under attack are flooded with stress hormones that minimize their pain perception and make them stronger and more effective at eluding predators. Even though animals cannot tell us these things for themselves, we can identify these effects in accounts from human beings who have experienced predator attack.

Achmat Hassiem's shark attack illustrates many aspects of the fight-or-flight response (Hassiem 2010). In 2006, Achmat was swimming off Sunrise Beach with his brother, Taariq. They were treading water during a life-saving exercise while two fellow lifeguards stayed in a boat nearer shore:

> Then something caught my eye – I looked around and saw a large shark fin darting towards my brother. . . . I shouted to the guys in the boat to get Taariq out. As they headed for him, I knew I had to do something to distract the shark, so I started slapping the water. It worked. But now the fin turned and came towards me. . . .
>
> I felt relieved that Taariq was safe, but scared because I was now the only person in the water. . . . Seconds later, a huge black shape rose up beside me. Its head was enormous, particularly the mouth – it looked big enough to walk

into. I was face to face with a 15 ft great white. I touched the shark with my
feet to try to push myself away, but that only sent it into a frenzy. . . .

It was nearly on me now, and my instinct was somehow to get on top of it.
I tried desperately to push myself up, but for some reason my right leg
wouldn't move. I looked down and saw why: everything below my knee
was in the shark's mouth. . . .

Then it took me underwater, still shaking me with my leg in its mouth.
I took a gulp and my lungs felt as if they were on fire. Then I got so angry,
I thought, "I'm not going down without a fight." I started attacking the shark
with all my remaining strength, grabbing its eye and punching its nose – I was
hitting it so much that when I reached hospital, there was no skin left on my
knuckles.

I could feel my body moving farther from its mouth as its teeth slid down
the bone towards my ankle. I gave one last enormous push and heard a great
snapping sound. Suddenly, I was free. I had been dragged about 50 m under
water and when I broke the surface I was close to blacking out.

The boat was nearer now, and Taariq saw me floating in the water. He
grabbed my hand and started pulling me out. As I looked back, I could see the
shark powering towards me, chewing what must have been my foot.
I collapsed into the boat as it brushed past. My brother had my injured leg
between his bicep and forearm, trying to stop the bleeding, and to shield me
from the extent of my injury.

I didn't know it, but halfway down my shin there was nothing left.

Thankfully, Achmat survived to compete with South Africa's national swimming team at the 2008 Beijing Paralympics. Yet, his experience provides an
excellent perspective of prey when attacked by a predator.

Achmat's sighting of the shark fin initiates the fear event that begins the
corresponding adrenal response and his SIA. Also notice Achmat's splashing
successfully distracted the shark from his brother because predators preferentially target prey in distress, which Achmat was simulating. Achmat is more
fearful once he is alone in the water, which keeps his stress hormones elevated.
Consequently, moments later when the shark attacks, he will not feel pain from
the event. Like most prey, Achmat first tries to flee. He tries to push away and
get on top of the shark, but is surprised he can't. He doesn't know why his right
leg won't move and must look down to visually ascertain his leg is clenched in
the shark's teeth. Notice Achmat's somatosensory cortex is working, telling him
his right leg is immobile, but his ACC is suppressed by endogenous opioids, so
he is unable to feel any pain associated with the injury. When Achmat is dragged
underwater, we observe the adrenal fight instinct of the cornered animal. He
feels anger, uses clear-headed strategies like grabbing the eye and punching the
nose, and continues to experience SIA as he punches the shark until the skin on
his knuckles is gone. In fact, the analgesia is so strong Achmat breaks his own

leg to free himself. Even when safely in the boat, his natural pain suppression is so great he doesn't realize his lower leg is gone.

Achmat is insensitive to his injuries because endogenous opioids from his pain suppression systems continue to operate throughout his ordeal and afterward like the long-term analgesic responses studied in rats. Researchers discovered the central nervous system has numerous pathways for pain suppression (Basbaum and Fields 1984). These involve opioid and non-opioid mechanisms which are anatomically and neurochemically distinct from each other (Watkins and Mayer 1982). When subjected to *inescapable* electric shock, rats demonstrated a short-term nonopioid analgesic response for approximately thirty minutes along with a longer-lasting opioid analgesic response lasting up to twenty-four hours after shocks ended (Maier et al. 1980; Grau et al. 1981; Maier 1989). However, rats allowed to escape shocks experienced no analgesia whatsoever (Grau et al. 1981: 1409). This suggests opioid-induced analgesia only occurs when subjects cannot evade or avoid the trauma. Achmat, who also found himself in an inescapable traumatic situation, appears to have experienced opioid-induced analgesia similar to rats that endured inescapable shock. Therefore, it is reasonable to conclude other mammals experience opioid-induced analgesia when they undergo inescapable predator attack, eliciting the strong endogenous pain suppression mechanisms that block pain perception for hours.

These examples of SIA demonstrate that human beings in otherwise safe environments experience pain differently than humans and mammals under duress (Fein 2014: 136). This may explain the observations of Harvard anesthesiologist Dr. Henry K. Beecher. Treating 215 casualties at Anzio beachhead in World War II, Beecher observed, "only one in four soldiers [25%] with serious injuries (fractures, amputations, penetrated chests or cerebrums) asked for morphine, though it was freely available. They simply did not need help with the pain, and indeed many of them denied feeling pain at all" (Brand and Yancey 1997: 203–204). Beecher compared soldiers' responses to injury to his patients in private practice, where 80 percent of patients healing from surgical wounds plead for morphine or other painkillers. These observations may be explained by the studies on rats exposed to inescapable shock. Like the opioid response of these rats, soldiers who faced the inescapable trauma of a battlefield environment would be far more likely to experience ongoing opioid-induced analgesia than patients undergoing (escapable) surgery in a hospital setting. Scholars therefore not only need to avoid anthropocentric assumptions about animal suffering in nature but must also be more self-aware that their protected comfortable environments and relative unfamiliarity with life-threatening fear makes them far less capable of correctly interpreting animal pain than they may realize.

The evidence suggests prey do not suffer from pain while they are fleeing and fighting to survive, but what about those moments near death? Surely, the kill bite must be painful? Again, as observers a safe distance from danger, we often assume this must be the case. Yet, empirical evidence does not appear to support this conclusion either. As observed for Achmat and the Anzio soldiers, the endogenous opioid system operates throughout the threatening episode and beyond. If exhaustion or asphyxiation leads to unconsciousness, as it nearly did for Achmat, it would leave the prey unaware of any additional attacks or injuries from predators. Also, many injuries in nature, whether caused by predation, sickness, or injury, can quickly initiate a life-threatening but opioid-releasing condition known as *shock*.

Shock can be caused by heavy bleeding (hemorrhagic/hypovolemic shock), damage to the spine (neurogenic shock), or infection entering the blood stream (septic shock) (State Government of Victoria, Australia 2014). Shock causes blood pressure to decrease, reducing the flow of oxygen and nutrients to the brain, heart, lungs, and other organs and, if not reversed, quickly leads to unconsciousness and death. Traumatic injury, hemorrhaging, and sepsis also activate the neuroendocrine and endogenous opiate systems, producing analgesia for critically wounded creatures (Molina 2003; 2006). Therefore, empirical evidence suggests creatures like the gazelle, who will die from tissue trauma and bleeding, experience analgesia both before and after the "kill bite."

Still, the speed of death is often dependent upon the age of the animal. Young animals can be killed so quickly by predators there is little chance for them to feel pain at all, especially if fear has already produced SIA. In contrast, more mature animals have greater skill and strength for eluding predators but may have to endure longer periods of fighting or fleeing as well, as in the case of a seal lion eluding killer whales or a zebra pursued by hyenas.

During such an encounter, as the animal depletes its glucose it begins showing symptoms of both neurogenic and neuroglycopenic hypoglycemia (Eysenck 2000: 172; Cryer 2007: 868–869). *Neurogenic hypoglycemia* occurs when glucose levels get dangerously low and activate the autonomic nervous system – symptoms include trembling, heart palpitations, nervousness, sweating, hunger, and tingling in the peripheral nerves. *Neuroglycopenic hypoglycemia* results from glucose blood concentrations dropping too low to fuel normal brain function – symptoms include confusion, a feeling of warmth, weakness/fatigue, drowsiness, severe cognitive failure, seizure, or coma (Towler et al. 1993; Cryer 1999).

So, when prey endure prolonged pursuit by predators who seek to exhaust them, their glucose levels decrease dramatically and can eventually result in measurable cognitive dysfunction and neuronal death (Blomqvist et al. 1991; Clarke and Sokoloff 1994; Aubert et al. 2005; Lubow et al. 2006; Schurr 2006; Cryer 2007: 868). It is therefore likely prey animals experiencing fatigue also begin to experience neuroglycopenic symptoms of disorientation, confusion, drowsiness, and cognitive failure associated with glucose depletion. Consequently, exhausted prey would simultaneously feel opioid-induced analgesia with loss of cognitive awareness and fear before being killed by their predators.

This combination effectively mimics Dawkins' "tranquilizing effect" that occurs when an animal has depleted its stores of glucose and no longer has the strength to fight or flee. In light of these findings, it may be time to reexamine metaphysical assertions of Nature's cruelty and indifference, and instead conclude that Nature may be much more concerned for the suffering of her creatures than it may appear on the surface.

4.4 Accounts of Cruel Animals

Philosophical claims of natural evil are frequently based upon incomplete representations of animal behavior. The predatory behaviors of orcas and accounts of avian siblicide have been prime examples of such misunderstandings. In these cases, poorly understood observations of animal behavior are used to suggest evolution has produced creatures that are cruel to the weak and inflict needless suffering upon other animals. Fortunately, scientific advances in environmental ecology and animal behavior can correct such misconceptions and offer insight into God's providential care in nature.

4.4.1 Understanding the Behavior of Killer Whales

Concerned with nonmoral evil in nature, Holmes Rolston cited the predatory practices of orcas (2003: 67): "Orcas catch sea lions for food, and play with them, tossing the struggling lions into the air, prolonging their agony. I do not fault the killer whales, but I might ask whether the nature is evil that, through natural selection, results in the nature of such beasts." Rolston claimed orcas torture their prey as they play with them, effectively "prolonging their agony." Christopher Southgate shared this impression of orca cruelty, using a *National Geographic* article to support Rolston's claim that some orcas have chosen a gratuitously vicious method of predation (2008: 45):

> Rolston describes the behavior of certain kinds of orca which, in killing sea lions, will toss their victims playfully in the air, prolonging their agony. This type of orca is so feared by its prey animals that dolphins will drag themselves

onto land and suffocate rather than face their predators [Chadwick 2005: 99].
As we consider this behavior, our focus may be on the orcas themselves. The
freedom of behavior involved in their lifestyle as predators can lead to what
seems to human observers like gratuitous infliction of suffering, but it does
not necessarily do so. Other types of orca do not show this behavior, and often
predators (unless teaching their young to hunt) kill their prey with the
minimum of energy and fuss.

Southgate appears to construe the behavior of mammal-consuming orcas as
though theirs is an intentionally cruel lifestyle that has been rejected by other
orcas. Unfortunately, Southgate misquoted the *National Geographic* article,
which actually states, "Dolphins are known to hurl themselves *up onto beach
rocks* in a suicidal frenzy to escape the mammal-hunting orcas" (Chadwick
2005: 99). Southgate's misquotation implies dolphins contemplate and deliber-
ately commit suicide as they "drag themselves onto land and suffocate rather
than face their predators" who would otherwise cause the "gratuitous infliction
of suffering." Setting aside the fact that beached dolphins die of dehydration and
not suffocation, this portrayal of the article does not faithfully convey the
complexity of orca behavior.

The *National Geographic* article actually explains (1) there are at least three
distinct subspecies of orca in the waters of North America's Pacific coast, (2)
they have not interbred for 10,000 years, and (3) orcas are actually the largest,
strongest, and brainiest dolphins in the world. These orca groups differ by diet,
"physical traits, travel patterns, social groupings, call patterns, and learned
traditions" (Chadwick 2005: 102).

Orcas that have evolved on a diet of fish, particularly salmon, remain close to
the Pacific shorelines and are referred to as *resident* orcas. A second subspecies
called *offshore* orcas are highly migratory, infrequently seen, and tend to be
smaller, feeding on a diet that includes sharks. The third orca subspecies living
off the Pacific coast feeds exclusively on warm-blooded mammals: seals, sea
otters, sea lions, porpoises, dolphins, and whales. These pods migrate greater
distances in search of prey and are therefore known as *transient* orcas.
Consequently, hunting behaviors differ between subspecies (Heimlich-Boran
1988: 565).

Resident orca pods call to each other freely with high-frequency pulses and
clicking while they hunt fish, openly broadcasting sonar in order to locate
salmon. Mammals like dolphins, porpoises, and sea lions swim alongside
resident orcas, recognizing they are not a threat.

In contrast, because transient orca pods hunt mammals that are more intelligent than fish, they must stalk their quarry more cautiously. They make longer
dives and directional feints, remain silent underwater, and send out only brief

sonar clicks that sound like stones knocking together in the surf to take their prey by surprise. This is why dolphins, otters, seals and sea lions may abruptly flee; transient orcas are their predators, residents are not. Therefore, it is a misrepresentation of the predator–prey dynamic to suggest mammals flee because transient orcas are cruel, rather than to acknowledge mammals flee when they recognize the presence of their predator.

It is also a distortion to suggest orcas cause "gratuitous infliction of suffering" by playing with their food, unnecessarily prolonging the agony of prey. Close observation of transient orcas reveals (1) there is no gratuitous delay between predator–prey encounter and prey death, and (2) transient orcas do not torment their food before eating it (Baird and Dill 1995). First, while orcas often engage in social-play behaviors, they only do so *after* a kill. Second, though young orcas have been observed increasing the handling time of their prey, or "play with their food," it is only *after* the prey is dead and during seasons (like the seal pupping period) when the immature orcas are especially well fed (Baird and Dill 1995: 1309). Researchers believe prolonged prey handling is linked to social-play behavior and is a necessary component of learning in young animals.

The importance of teaching juvenile killer whales how to hunt and handle prey should not be underestimated. The pod must ensure young orcas are capable of catching food for themselves before their mother's milk stops. This is why both resident and transient adult orcas are observed to pursue, but not kill, prey animals as they teach their young to hunt. A resident orca mother was witnessed herding a coho salmon without catching it until her calf finally captured it in its own jaws (Chadwick 2005: 104). Transient orca pod members demonstrated to juveniles and calves how to create waves to break up ice floes, separate them from other large pieces of ice, and wash prey (seals and penguins) off the ice into the water (Visser et al. 2008).

Stunning prey is another technique used by many subspecies of orca and passed down through family groups (Main 2015). Young orcas have observed their elders encircling a school of herring in open water, forcing fish into a tightly swimming ball (Chadwick 2005: 104). In this tactic, called carousel feeding, the whales take turns striking the circling ball of fish with their flukes, "stunning mouthful after mouthful." Orcas around New Zealand and Papua New Guinea have been spotted stunning sharks with their tails, rendering the otherwise dangerous prey dazed and harmless (Daily Mail Reporter 2009). This stunning technique is also used on marine mammals, as University of London evolutionary ecologist Rüdiger Riesch explains (Main 2015):

> A lot of marine mammals, like seals and sea lions, have very sharp claws and teeth, so killer whales are at risk of suffering a severe injury when hunting

these prey. Therefore, the safest course of action is for the killer whales to
debilitate their prey before getting anywhere near them. To do this they use
a combination of rams, often head-on, and slapping the prey with their flukes,
or tail fins. This can go on for 30 minutes or more, until the seal or sea lion is
too injured to fight back or potentially already dead.

It is the tail-strikes that sometimes toss the prey animals into the air. This
"flipping ability" is a learned hunting technique, stunning the prey into an
unconscious or semiconscious state. Steve Ferguson, an evolutionary ecologist
studying Arctic mammals with the University of Manitoba, points out "this
behavior has been attributed to mothers teaching their young how to hunt, [to
make] the prey easier targets" (Main 2015). It is this behavior Rolston claimed
was "evil," not understanding that this was one of the safest ways adult orcas
and their young could handle dangerous prey animals.

It should be remembered that orcas, like other predators, target weak, sickly,
or distressed members of prey populations, effectively minimizing suffering
within that population. Additionally, marine mammals – like land mammals –
engage their adrenal systems during times of predator attack, effectively flooding their brains with analgesic opioids. This means marine prey animals are
experiencing SIA even as they are being pursued by orcas. Furthermore, any
animal stunned by orca tail-strike(s) will likely be either unconscious or semiconscious when the kill bite occurs, minimizing their experience of pain before
death. It is therefore difficult to see how orca behaviors can be accurately
described as either needlessly cruel or evil.

4.4.2 Understanding Avian Siblicide

Avian siblicide is observed among some predatory species where a chick kills
its sibling by forcing it out of the nest to die of exposure, being so aggressive the
weaker chick does not eat and dies of starvation, or pecking it until it dies (Mock
et al. 1990). Rolston described avian siblicide and criticized it as an inefficient
method of reproduction that causes unnecessary suffering and appears to exhibit
an uncaring indifference toward the hapless chick (1987: 137–140). He sadly
but understandably concluded: "If God watches the sparrows fall, God must do
so from a great distance."

Nevertheless, additional scientific information shows Nature is not always as
she seems. To begin, avian siblicide is a form of brood reduction only observed
in predatory altricial bird species: eagles, ospreys, boobies, egrets, and pelicans.
The two forms of avian siblicide observed are *facultative* – which only occurs
when food resources are scarce – and *obligate* – which occurs when other
predators are scarce.

Altricial birds (like eagles, hawks, owls, songbirds, and doves) are those whose hatchlings require intensive parental care and provision as they are unable to stand, walk, fly, or survive independently. In contrast, *precocial* birds (like chickens, turkeys, and ducks) are well developed at hatching and are able to stand, walk, leave the nest, and feed themselves shortly after birth. Precocial and altricial birds have each made an evolutionary trade-off when it comes to reproductive costs and timing of neurological development (Ehrlich, Dobkin, and Wheye 1988). This divergence is due to differences in food availability and predation pressures in the birds' respective environments.

Precocial birds nest on or near the ground where predation and food resources are both greatest. Faced with greater predation pressure, their young must be capable of leaving the nest almost immediately after hatching, avoiding easy predation and the possibility of the entire brood being devoured at once. In order to produce developmentally mature hatchlings that can fend for themselves, precocial females consume abundant resources *before* laying and the nutrition consumed will determine how many eggs can be laid. These large energy-rich eggs enable substantial in-egg growth of their developmentally advanced chicks. Therefore, most brain development occurs before hatching and precocial chicks will have nearly the same number of brain neurons as adults, just packed with greater density (Iwaniuk and Nelson 2003). Consequently, precocial chicks are hatched with much larger, more advanced brains than altricial chicks, enabling precocial chicks to be relatively independent at an early age.

In contrast, altricial birds tend to nest off the ground, reducing both predation pressures and food resources. Because hatchlings will not need to be as developmentally mature at birth, females require less nutrition before they lay their eggs, with altricial eggs containing only half the calories per unit weight of precocial eggs. Consequently, altricial chicks are born with much smaller underdeveloped brains than precocial chicks (Starck 1993; Iwaniuk and Nelson 2003: 1924). Although altricial chick brains are initially neurologically underdeveloped, this deficiency is overcome if their parents can provide the protein-rich diet typical of these species (Ehrlich, Dobkin, and Wheye 1988).

Because altricial chick survival depends upon parental ability to provide food after hatching, annual food abundance is a determinative factor on the species' reproductive success. Consequently, while various forms of altricial brood reduction may seem inefficient on a superficial level, they actually maximize the number of offspring that can be successfully fledged in any given year.

Oxford ornithologist David Lack recognized that in order to increase the chances of producing one or more fledged chicks in uncertain food environments, some altricial bird species evolved with the strategy of laying more eggs than they may successfully provide for, with the female creating competitive mismatches among broodmates via asynchronous hatching and different sized eggs (1947; 1948). These factors are especially important for understanding avian siblicide.

The (first) *a*-egg is typically much larger and hatches 1–3 days before the smaller (second) *b*-egg, giving the *a*-chick several days to grow larger as it monopolizes all food the parents bring to the nest. Because the smaller egg contains far fewer lipids and nutrients, chicks from smaller *b*-eggs display suppressed growth rates, delayed development of feathers, and increased mortality rates both before and after fledging (Wiebe and Bortolotti 2000: 2). Taken together, the separation of hatching dates compounded by differences in egg size means *a*-chicks may weigh two to three times more than *b*-chicks when they finally hatch (Mock 1984: 13).

However, it is important to note the *a*-egg/chick will not necessarily live to fledging; eggs can be stolen or infertile, and additional factors may kill or weaken it before the second chick hatches (hence the evolutionary need for a second "insurance" chick). Researchers consistently find the probability of producing at least one fledging chick is greater for two-chick nests than one-chick nests (Mock 1984: 14). Black eagles produced a fledged chick only 49.0 percent of the time with one egg, but 76.4 percent of the time with an insurance chick. More strikingly, masked boobies with one egg fledged a chick only 20 percent of the time whereas two-chick nests had a fledging rate of 63 percent.

Asynchronous hatching and egg-size disparities actually maximize the number of offspring successfully fledged in any given year while minimizing harm that would come to both chicks if they were at identical stages of development in the nest. Researchers discovered this through experimental interventions where cattle egret siblings hatched on the same day (synchronously) were compared to chicks hatched at the normal 1.5-day interval, and chicks hatched with a longer 3-day interval between hatchings (Mock et al. 1990: 445). The synchronized hatchlings, being comparable in size, demonstrated more fighting and higher mortality for both broodmates. Nests with the normal 1.5-day interval had less fighting because the older *a*-chick was able to intimidate the younger *b*-chick and get more food, yet the *b*-chick was still able to eat. The chicks hatched with the longer 3-day interval had the least fighting, but the *a*-chick was so competitively over-advantaged that the *b*-chick received very little food. Therefore, rather than being an inefficient method of reproduction, it appears evolution has tuned the asynchronous hatching and differential egg size of these altricial birds so both chicks' chances for survival have been optimized.

Just because *b*-chicks are at a competitive disadvantage does not mean their deaths are inevitable. Most cases of avian siblicide are *facultative*, meaning the weaker *b*-chicks die only in times of food scarcity or weather conditions hinder adults' foraging. In abundant years, adult birds spend less time obtaining food and more time in the nest. There they intervene against sibling aggression by dividing the brood between parents, separating offspring at feeding, offering more frequent feedings, clustering meals, prolonging feedings to distract nestlings, and/or preferentially feeding weaker nestlings (Wiebe and Bortolotti 2000: 2, 5). Acute parental responses to aggression can include physical interventions with adults blocking, pecking, grabbing, or sitting on the aggressive nestling. Under these conditions, *b*-chicks can obtain sufficient nutrition to fully develop and fledge the nest. However, when food is scarce, adults will often be absent and nutrition will be insufficient to fledge both chicks, with the *b*-chick remaining developmentally delayed, frail, and vulnerable to sickness, injury, and starvation. Studies also show in times of scarcity the *a*-chick's aggressive tendencies toward its sibling increase with hunger (White et al. 2010). Under these circumstances, facultative siblicide occurs.

The rarer form of siblicide is *obligate* (Mock et al. 1990: 441). Unlike *facultative* siblicide, which depends upon environmental factors affecting food availability, *obligate* siblicide almost always results in the death of the weaker *b*-chick in species that have few to no natural predators, like eagles in remote nests and boobies on isolated islands. While gulls sometimes consume booby eggs and the youngest of hatchlings, gape-limitation prevents them from swallowing hatchlings more than a couple of days old. Consequently, no other form of predation is available to eliminate sick or weakly chicks, so it appears natural selection has chosen the stronger of the two predatory siblings to fulfill this role. This observation is supported by the fact that obligate siblicide appears to decrease among birds of prey as their size decreases and susceptibility to ordinary predation increases (Newton 1977; Mock 1984: 17).

Therefore, while obligate siblicide fulfills the predator's role and terminates the lives of malnourished chicks in less accessible locations, it is fair to ask, "Even though predation is intended to minimize suffering and distress, doesn't the pecking and/or starvation associated with siblicide cause unnecessary suffering in chicks before they die?" The best answer seems to be, "No, it does not."

To understand this answer, it is important to recognize how altricial chicks' underdeveloped brains hinder their ability to perceive pain. Research shows the telencephalic region of the bird forebrain regulates social behavior and pain perception like the ACC found in mammals (Goodson 2005; Jarvis et al. 2005; Jarvis 2009; Güntürkün and Bugnyar 2016; Scheiber et al. 2017). However, while precocial chicks demonstrate pain perception, this is because their neural networks are nearly as developed as precocial adults (Panksepp et al. 1980; Iwaniuk and Nelson 2003). In contrast, altricial chicks lack both cellular differentiation and myelination of axons that allow efficient transfer of neurological signals in the brain. Therefore, since brain development only occurs with the consumption of nutrient-rich food *after* hatching, it is reasonable to conclude malnourished *b*-chicks who are victims of siblicide have brains too neurocognitively underdeveloped to perceive the distressing aspect of pain. Studies on post-fledging neural and behavioral development confirm most neurological development in altricial birds occurs after birds leave the nest, and until that time their neurocognitive abilities are lacking compared to either precocial chicks or altricial adults (Iwaniuk and Nelson 2003: 1925).

The absence of pain perception in undernourished, developmentally delayed chicks is expected because pain is only an evolutionary advantage for animals capable of learning. Since these chicks have not achieved sufficient physical and neurological development to allow them to learn from or respond to negative stimuli, it would be premature for them to experience pain. Unsurprisingly, chicks pecked by siblings often exhibit responses resembling indifference to pain and injury. Furthermore, research shows aggression between chicks decreases dramatically as they develop and mature, suggesting that as the neurocognitive likelihood of pain perception increases, the natural instinct to attack nest mates decreases (Wiebe and Bortolotti 2000: 3). So, instead of being a source of needless suffering, avian siblicide in altricial birds ensures chicks who will not survive to fledging are removed *before* they can feel pain from either starvation, exposure, or injury. This provides another example of God's providential concern for every creature, where not even a sparrow can fall to the ground outside of God's care (Matt 10:29), and leaves the accusation that God displays an uncaring indifference toward these hapless chicks considerably weakened.

4.4.3 Accusations of Animal Immorality Contradict Atheists' Worldview

Before proceeding, it should not go unnoticed the reason the insurance chick is selected over other examples of chick death is because of the issue of *siblicide.* Implicit in this selection is the understandable anthropocentric belief that it is morally wrong to kill either one's child or family member. Yet, neither the five-day old cattle egret nor its younger sibling have any such abstract notions of familial love, social cohesion, or betrayal. Therefore, to claim animals are behaving in morally inappropriate ways is to impose human value systems onto nonhuman creatures and shift away from claims of natural evil to moral evil.

Atheists are not on firm footing when they insinuate it's morally wrong for an adult lion to kill cubs or for a young chick to kill its sibling because their assertion contains a contradiction of their own worldview. First, to claim situations exist where it is morally wrong for one animal to kill another appeals to the notion that there is some universal standard of morality even animals must acknowledge. If such a standard exists, where does it come from? What is its source? Can it be deduced from the characteristics of atoms or wavelengths of light? No, quite the contrary. Morality is not a property of matter, so atheists (who also tend to be metaphysical naturalists/materialists) are arguing for the existence of something that cannot be supported by their worldview. Second, even if atheists concede there is a universal standard of morality that animals created by God should be expected to abide by, the theist can easily point out only moral agents are capable of recognizing and adhering to moral standards of behavior. This is why young children are not held to the same standard of behavior as adults; they do not yet have the neurocognitive maturity necessary for adult moral behavior (Blocher 1984: 132). Therefore, to contend it is reasonable to expect moral behavior from animals, atheists must show nonhuman creatures along the evolutionary spectrum have evolved the neurocognitive capacity to recognize the difference between moral and immoral behavior. Then, if atheists do manage to show nonhuman creatures are capable of discerning moral from immoral behavior, they must explain how "random" non-teleological evolutionary processes produced a universal, nonrelativistic standard of morality.

In contrast, theists can argue that while there is a universal standard of morality, nonhuman animals are not moral agents as human beings are, and although some mammals may demonstrate intra- and extra-species kindness, protection, and empathy, this does not mean they should be judged by the same behavioral standards as human beings. Furthermore, many philosophers overlook the fact that Scripture describes three categories of moral behavior: *moral* (associated with justice), *immoral* (associated with injustice), and *nonmoral* (associated with non-justice) (Tsevat 1980: 37). Animal predation and aggressive behaviors fall into the nonmoral category since nonhumans are not moral agents according to biblical standards (Werther and Linville 2012: 162). As nonmoral agents, animals are neither aware of notions of justice, nor do they perceive themselves as victims of injustice. Such concepts are not a part of their reality and therefore can neither enhance nor detract from their existence. In light of this, it becomes readily apparent the atheistic worldview has fewer conceptual resources to respond to notions of "immoral" animal behavior than theism.

5 Re-evaluating the Evidential Problem of Natural Evil

After the preceding analysis, the following conclusions may be drawn:

1. It is inaccurate to claim starvation and misery represent the normal state of creatures in nature since natural systems move toward equilibrium states (ecological balance between population and food supply) rather than disequilibrium states (perpetual hunger).

2. It is inappropriate to treat creaturely sufferings as quantifiable units that can be summed to show God does not love his creatures. This is a category error because creaturely suffering is a qualitative subjective experience and cannot be summed any more than creaturely pleasure. As a subjective experience, suffering must be understood and comforted on an individual basis.

3. Just as it is logically impossible to create a square circle, it appears to be biologically impossible to create long-lived, thinking, task-oriented creatures without including an internalized, pain-driven warning system. Pain is biologically necessary among more highly evolved creatures capable of learning. The perception of pain increases the likelihood of a creature's survival and its healthy longevity. Creatures that cannot feel or learn from their pain and pleasure experiences will be more likely to die prematurely.

4. It is misleading to suggest most creatures produced by evolutionary processes are capable of suffering. Empirical evidence establishes 98.4 percent of all animal species on earth are invertebrates and lack the psychological ability to feel pain. In fact, the National Academy of Sciences has concluded evidence for the conscious experience of pain is only strong for mammals and birds. Therefore, it is irresponsible for philosophers to continue to cite less highly evolved species that are neurocognitively incapable of perceiving pain as their illustrations of cruelty in nature.

5. It is a significant misrepresentation to suggest that for millions of years on earth most creatures have spent the bulk of their lives suffering horribly. First, only 0.5 percent of all species have the neurocognitive capacity to experience suffering. Second, of those who begin to suffer when their health deteriorates, predators quickly detect and dispatch them while the prey animal's brain is flooded with endogenous opioids, effectively minimizing the experience of pain in nature. That is why the claim animal existence is "dominated by pain" is both exceedingly misleading as well as poorly reasoned. Chronic pain would diminish, not enhance, the ability of creatures to survive, so it is a trait one would expect to be eliminated by natural selection and prevented from being passed down to following generations. Third, the creatures that can feel pain, namely mammals and birds, are social creatures who are able to mitigate one another's pain through empathetic relationships, recognized as the *brain opioid theory of social attachment*.

6. Empirical evidence does not support the claim that creatures endure unnecessary suffering from parasites, disease and predator attack. Scientific studies confirm predators have evolved to recognize and preferentially prey upon

animals who begin to show the earliest signs of physical distress due to parasites, disease, or injury. Those creatures with the capacity for pain also possess adrenal systems that release endogenous opioids and other stress hormones when they are under predator attack that help them survive and suppress pain until the animal is no longer pursued or has been killed.

In fact, by Richard Dawkins' own criteria, it would be reasonable to claim Nature is *not* indifferent to suffering since it appears unnecessary suffering in creation has been minimized to a very great extent. This is consistent with the theist's worldview that a loving, benevolent God created a beautiful world shaped with providential care for all its creatures.

5.1 Revisiting Rowe's Evidential Problem of Natural Evil

It is therefore fair for the theist to conclude claims of cruelty in nature have been considerably weakened. First, empirical evidence suggests suffering is *not* widespread across the evolutionary spectrum and is curtailed far more than previously assumed. Second, *without pain perception more highly evolved long-lived species with greater intelligence would be unlikely to exist, their nonexistence being an evil equally bad or worse than existence with pain perception.* Together, these two conclusions greatly diminish Rowe's evidential premise (1) – *an omnipotent, omniscient being could have prevented unnecessary suffering without thereby losing some greater good or permitting some evil equally bad or worse.*

In premise (2) Rowe claimed an omniscient, wholly good being would prevent unnecessary suffering in nature. This is another widely shared assumption among nontheists regarding the purposes of God, but it too is vulnerable to serious critique. First, scientific evidence suggests unnecessary suffering in nature *has* been prevented. Second, Rowe and Draper incorrectly imagine an omniscient, wholly good being would adopt their value system of hedonistic utilitarianism, which assumes pleasure and biological success are the greatest goods while pain and biological failure are the greatest harms. Instead, the value system of the biblical Judeo-Christian God is one of love and evidenced in nature by the mitigation of pain through empathetic social interactions and the release of endogenous opioids during traumatic and/or life-threatening situations. In other words, the omniscient, omnipotent, wholly good and loving God of the theist has created a world filled with God's providential care, which minimizes the suffering of creatures even in the midst of injury and death. Consequently, Rowe's premise (2) that asserts an omniscient, wholly good being would not allow suffering is inaccurate.

Therefore, since premises (1) and (2) are faulty, Rowe's conclusion (3) "there does not exist an omnipotent, omniscient, wholly good being" is also unsound.

5.2 Seeking the Best Explanation

In this section, the comparative approach *inference to the best explanation* will evaluate Draper's hypothesis of indifference against the Judeo-Christian hypothesis of theism to determine which is more probable. The question is, "Does the Judeo-Christian hypothesis of theism have more or less explanatory and predictive power than the hypothesis of indifference?" For this comparison, the two philosophical hypotheses will be evaluated like scientific hypotheses are where the superior hypothesis is the one that deals with the most evidence, has the greater explanatory power, and correctly anticipates outcomes.

The Judeo-Christian hypothesis of theism:

- Anticipates a finely tuned and *ordered* cosmos defined by natural laws and described with mathematical precision. The concept of an ordered universe is conveyed in ANE understandings of Genesis 1 as well as the rhetoric found in texts like Psalm 104, Proverbs 8:12–31, and Job 38:4–18.
- Anticipates a *telos* in the universe that would enable life to evolve from nonlife so creatures could have fellowship with God. This worldview also explains why Earth's most highly evolved creatures, humans made in the image of God (Gen 1:26–27), would have the capacity to comprehend the order of the cosmos.
- Anticipates and explains why human beings would have an innate sense of *morality*.
- Anticipates and explains why human beings would have desire for relationship with the divine through *religion* and/or other spiritual practices.
- Anticipates a loving God would minimize unnecessary *suffering* among creatures in nature.
- Anticipates and explains why *empathetic love* would reduce suffering among creatures that feel pain.

In contrast, the hypothesis of indifference states "neither the nature nor the condition of sentient beings on earth is the result of benevolent or malevolent actions performed by non-human persons" (Draper 1989: 332). What does this hypothesis anticipate? Nothing. What does it explain? Nothing. This "hypothesis" is the statement of a negative that cannot be tested. Even if one is supposed to assume by "indifference" that 50/50 random chance is meant, such a hypothesis would predict an ordered universe was as likely as a disordered universe. Evolutionary existence would be as probable as nonexistence. The hypothesis of an indifferent universe would anticipate sentience with equal probability as nonsentience. In fact, the hypothesis of indifference can predict and explain . . . nothing at all.

Atheism's greatest strength has been that Western theism, based upon Greco-Roman interpretations of Genesis 1–3, was incompatible with neo-Darwinian evolution and Earth's geological history (Plantinga 2011: 3–63). However, since alternative interpretations are available that incorporate ANE insights and remove purported conflicts between science and the Genesis text (Section 2.4), Judeo-Christian theism is wholly compatible with evolution even as atheism fails to provide the explanatory power it claims. In short, the Judeo-Christian worldview can offer a scientifically tenable explanation of suffering in a neo-Darwinian world that makes the hypothesis of theism more probable than the hypothesis of indifference.

References

Adams, Marilyn McCord (1999). *Horrendous Evils and the Goodness of God*, Ithaca, NY: Cornell University Press.

American Veterinary Medical Association (2020). *AVMA Guidelines for the Euthanasia of Animals: 2020 Edition*. Online: www.avma.org/sites/default/files/2020-02/Guidelines-on-Euthanasia-2020.pdf (accessed October 24, 2022).

Arnold, Bill T. (2013). *Genesis*, New Cambridge Bible Commentary, New York: Cambridge University Press.

Arnold, Bill T., and Brent A. Strawn, eds. (2016). *The World Around the Old Testament: The People and Places of the Ancient Near East*, Grand Rapids, MI: Baker Academic.

Aronson, Dina (2009). "Cortisol – Its Role in Stress, Inflammation, and Indications for Diet Therapy," *Today's Dietitian* 11, 38. Online: www.todaysdietitian.com/newarchives/111609p38.shtml (accessed October 9, 2017).

Aubert, Agnès, Robert Costalat, Pierre J. Magistretti, and Luc Pellerin (2005). "Brain Lactate Kinetics: Modeling Evidence for Neuronal Lactate Uptake upon Activation," *Proceedings of the National Academy of Sciences of the United States of America* 102, 16448–16453.

Augustine (1982). *The Literal Meaning of Genesis*, Ancient Christian Writers 41–42, John H. Taylor (trans.), 2 vols., New York: Newman.

Baird, Robin W., and Lawrence M. Dill (1995). "Occurrence and Behaviour of Transient Killer Whales: Seasonal and Pod-Specific Variability, Foraging Behavior, and Prey Handling," *Canadian Journal of Zoology* 73, 1300–1311.

Barbour, Ian G. (1997). *Religion and Science: Historical and Contemporary Issues*, San Francisco: HarperCollins.

Barkley, Yvonne (2019). "Wildfire and Wildlife Habitat" (27 August), U.S. Cooperative Extension website. Online: https://surviving-wildfire.extension.org/wildfire-and-wildlife-habitat/#Wildlife_and_Fire (accessed August 31, 2022).

Basbaum, Allan I., and Howard L. Fields (1984). "Endogenous Pain Control Systems: Brainstem Spinal Pathways and Endorphin Circuitry," *Annual Review of Neuroscience* 7, 309–338.

Basbaum, Allan I., Diana M. Bautista, Grégory Scherrer, and David Julius (2009). "Cellular and Molecular Mechanisms of Pain," *Cell* 139, 267–284.

Bimson, John J. (2006). "Reconsidering a 'Cosmic Fall'," *Science & Christian Belief* 18, 63–81.

Birnbaum, Philip (1975). *A Book of Jewish Concepts*, New York: Hebrew Publishing.

Blocher, Henri (1984). *In the Beginning: The Opening Chapters of Genesis*, David G. Preston (trans.), Leicester: InterVarsity.

Blomqvist, Gunnar, Albert Gjedde, Mark Gutniak et al. (1991). "Facilitated Transport of Glucose from Blood to Brain in Man and the Effect of Moderate Hypoglycaemia on Cerebral Glucose Utilization," *European Journal of Nuclear Medicine* **18**, 834–837.

Bonnet, V. H., Anna W. Schoettle, and Wayne D. Shepperd (2005). "Postfire Environmental Conditions Influence the Spatial Pattern of Regeneration for *Pinus ponderosa*," *Canadian Journal of Forest Research* **35**, 37–47.

Borsook, David, Eric A. Moulton, Karl F. Schmidt, and Lino R. Becerra (2007). "Neuroimaging Revolutionizes Therapeutic Approaches to Chronic Pain," *Molecular Pain* **3**, no pages.

Boyd, Gregory A. (2001) *Satan and the Problem of Evil: Constructing a Trinitarian Warfare Theodicy*, Downers Grove, IL: InterVarsity.

Brand, Paul, and Philip Yancey (1997). *The Gift of Pain: Why We Hurt and What We Can Do About It*, Grand Rapids, MI: Zondervan.

Brown, Matthew (2012). "Dead Livestock, Devastation Left in Wake of Western Fires," *Billings Gazette* (July 26). Online: http://billingsgazette .com/news/state-and-regional/montana/dead-livestock-devastation-left-in-wake-of-western-fires/article_48f1f91d-d247-5df4-8ff1-78dee1f9d93d .html (accessed January 21, 2017).

Bruce, Frederick F. (1963). *The Epistle of Paul to the Romans*, Tyndale New Testament Commentaries, London: Tyndale.

Buckareff, Andrei (2000). "Divine Freedom and Creaturely Suffering in Process Theology: A Critical Appraisal," *Sophia* **39**, 56–69.

Butler, Ryan K., and David P. Finn (2009). "Stress-Induced Analgesia," *Progress in Neurobiology* **88**, 184–202.

Calvin, John (1849). *Commentaries on the Epistle of Paul to the Romans*, Christian Classics Ethereal Library, John Owen (trans., ed.), Edinburgh: Calvin Translation Society. Online: www.ccel.org/ccel/calvin/calcom38 .xii.vi.html (accessed August 31, 2022).

Canada Senate Standing Committee on Legal and Constitutional Affairs (CSSCLCA) (2003a). "Proceedings of the Standing Senate Committee on Legal and Constitutional Affairs, Issue 7 – Evidence for February 12, 2003," Senate of Canada website. Online: https://sencanada.ca/en/Content/SEN/ Committee/372/lega/07eva-e?Language=EandParl=37andSes=2andcomm_ id=11 (accessed August 31, 2022).

(2003b) "Do Invertebrates Feel Pain?" Senate of Canada website. Online: https://sencanada.ca/content/sen/committee/372/lega/witn/shelly-e.htm (accessed August 31, 2022).

Casey, Kenneth L., and Tuan D. Tran (2006). "Cortical Mechanisms Mediating Acute and Chronic Pain in Humans." In Fernando Cervero and Troels S. Jensen (eds.), *Pain*. Vol. 81 of *Handbook of Clinical Neurology*, Amsterdam: Elsevier, pp. 159–177.

Cervero, Fernando, and Harold Merskey (1996). "What Is a Noxious Stimulus?" *The Journal of Pain* **5**, 157–161.

Chadwick, Douglas H. (2005). "Investigating a Killer," *National Geographic* **207**, 86–105.

Chang, Chi-Ru (1996). "Ecosystem Responses to Fire and Variations in Fire Regimes," *Sierra Nevada Ecosystem Project: Final Report to Congress*. Vol. II of *Assessments and Scientific Basis for Management Options*, Davis: University of California, Centers for Water and Wildland Resources, pp. 1071–1099.

Chavalas, Mark W., and K. Lawson Younger Jr., eds. (2002). *Mesopotamia and the Bible: Comparative Explorations*, Grand Rapids, MI: Baker Academic.

Church of Satan website. Online: www.churchofsatan.com/ (accessed May 21, 2021).

Clarke, Donald D., and Louis Sokoloff (1994). "Circulation and Energy Metabolism of the Brain." In George J. Siegel, Bernard W. Agranoff, R. Wayne Albers, and Perry B. Molinoff (eds.), *Basic Neurochemistry: Molecular, Cellular and Medical Aspects*, New York: Raven, pp. 645–680.

Creegan, Nicola H. (2013). *Animal Suffering and the Problem of Evil*, Oxford: Oxford University Press.

Cryer, Philip E. (1999). "Symptoms of Hypoglycemia, Thresholds for Their Occurrence, and Hypoglycemia Unawareness," *Endocrinology Metabolism Clinics of North America* **28**, 495–500.

(2007) "Hypoglycemia, Functional Brain Failure, and Brain Death," *Journal of Clinical Investigation* **117**, 868–870.

Daily Mail Reporter (2009). "Pictured: The Moment a Whale Delivers a Deadly 'Karate Chop' Blow to a Killer Shark," *Daily Mail* (November 27). Online: www.dailymail.co.uk/sciencetech/article-1231454/Killer-whales-Death-karate-chop-deadly-tactic-used-orcas-sharks.html (accessed July 16, 2022).

Darwin, Charles (2009). *On the Origin of Species: By Means of Natural Selection*, 6th ed., Auckland: Floating Press.

Dawkins, Richard (2008). *River Out of Eden*, New York: Basic Books.

Deane-Drummond, Celia (2008). "Shadow Sophia in Christological Perspective: The Evolution of Sin and the Redemption of Nature," *Theology & Science* **6**, 13–32.

(2009). *Christ and Evolution: Wonder and Wisdom*, Minneapolis, MN: Fortress.

Delumeau, Jean (2000). *History of Paradise: The Garden of Eden in Myth and Tradition*, Matthew O'Connell (trans.), Champaign: University of Illinois Press.

Dougherty, Trent (2014). *The Problem of Animal Pain: A Theodicy for All Creatures Great and Small*, New York: Palgrave Macmillan.

Draper, Paul (1989). "Pain and Pleasure: An Evidential Problem for Theists," *Noûs* **23**, 331–350.

(2007) "Natural Selection and the Problem of Evil," Secular Web: Internet Infidels website. Online: https://infidels.org/library/modern/paul_draper/evil.html (accessed August 31, 2022).

Dunbar, Robin I. M. (2003). "The Social Brain: Mind, Language, and Society in Evolutionary Perspective," *Annual Review of Anthropology* **32**, 163–181.

Ehrlich, Paul R., David S. Dobkin, and Darryl Wheye (1988). "Precocial and Altricial Young," Stanford University website. Online: https://web.stanford.edu/group/stanfordbirds/text/essays/Precocial_and_Altricial.html (accessed July 16, 2022).

Eisemann, Craig H., Wayne K., Jorgensen, David J. Merritt et al. (1984). "Do Insects Feel Pain? – A Biological View," *Experientia* **40**, 164–167.

Engstrom, R. Todd (2010). "First-Order Fire Effects on Animals: Review and Recommendations," *Fire Ecology* **6**, 115–130.

Estes, James A., John Terborgh, Justin S. Brashares et al. (2011). "Trophic Downgrading of Planet Earth," *Science* **333**, 301–306.

Eysenck, Michael W. (2000). *Psychology: A Student's Handbook*. Hove, East Sussex: Psychology.

Febbraio, Mark A., D. L. Lambert, Rebecca L. Starkie, Joseph Proietto, and Mark Hargreaves (1998). "Effect of Epinephrine on Muscle Glycogenolysis during Exercise in Trained Men," *Journal of Applied Physiology* **84**, 465–470.

Fein, Alan (2014). "Nociceptors and the Perception of Pain." Online: https://health.uconn.edu/cell-biology/wp-content/uploads/sites/115/2017/10/Revised-Book-2014.pdf (accessed July 12, 2022).

Foltz, Eldon L., and Lowell E. White Jr. (1962). "Pain 'Relief' by Frontal Cingulumotomy," *Journal of Neurosurgery* **19**, 89–100.

Garland, Eric L. (2012). "Pain Processing in the Human Nervous System: A Selective Review of Nociceptive and Biobehavioral Pathways," *Primary Care: Clinics in Office Practice* **39**, 561–571.

Genovart, Meritxell, Nieves Negre, Giacomo Tavecchia et al. (2010). "The Young, the Weak and the Sick: Evidence of Natural Selection by Predation," *PLoS ONE* **5**, e9774.

Gleitman, Henry, James Gross, and Daniel Reisberg (2010). *Psychology*, 8th ed., New York: W. W. Norton.

Goodson, James L. (2005). "The Vertebrate Social Behavior Network: Evolutionary Themes and Variations," *Hormones and Behavior* **48**, 11–22.

Grau, James W., Richard L. Hyson, Steven F. Maier, John Madden IV, and Jack D. Barchas (1981). "Long-Term Stress-Induced Analgesia and Activation of the Opiate System," *Science* **213**, 1409–1411.

Green, Joel B. (2017). "Adam, What Have You Done?" In William T. Cavanaugh and James K. Smith (eds.), *Evolution and the Fall*, Grand Rapids, MI: Eerdmans, pp. 98–116.

Griffin, David R. (1981). "Creation Out of Chaos and the Problem of Evil." In Stephen T. Davis (ed.), *Encountering Evil: Live Options in Theodicy*, Edinburgh: T & T Clark, pp. 101–136.

  (2004) *God, Power, and Evil: A Process Theodicy*, Louisville, KY: Westminster John Knox.

Gunkel, Hermann (1997). *Genesis*, Mark E. Biddle (trans.), Macon, GA: Mercer University Press.

  (2006) *Creation and Chaos in the Primeval Era and the Eschaton: A Religio-Historical Study of Genesis 1 and Revelation 12*, K. William Whitney, Jr. (trans.), Grand Rapids, MI: Eerdmans.

Güntürkün, Onur, and Thomas Bugnyar (2016). "Cognition Without Cortex," *Trends in Cognitive Sciences* **20**, 291–303.

Halloran, John A. (2006). *Sumerian Lexicon: A Dictionary Guide to the Ancient Sumerian Language.* Los Angeles, CA: Logogram.

Hamilton, Victor P. (1990). *The Book of Genesis: Chapters 1–17*, New International Commentary on the Old Testament, Roland K. Harrison and Robert L. Hubbard (eds.), Grand Rapids, MI: Eerdmans.

Hanlon, Roger T., and John B. Messenger (1996). *Cephalopod Behaviour*, Cambridge: University of Cambridge Press.

Harrison, Peter (1989). "Theodicy and Animal Pain," *Philosophy* **64**, 79–92.

Hartshorne, Charles (1984). *Omnipotence and Other Theological Mistakes*, Albany, NY: SUNY Press.

Hassiem, Achmat (2010). "Experience: A Great White Shark Ate My Leg," *The Guardian* (October 15). Online: www.theguardian.com/lifeandstyle/2010/oct/16/experience-shark-attack-paralympian (accessed July 15, 2022).

Heimlich-Boran, James R. (1988). "Behavioral Ecology of Killer Whales (*Orcinus orca*) in the Pacific Northwest," *Canadian Journal of Zoology* **66**, 565–578.

Hesiod (2008). *Theogony and Works and Days*, Martin L. West (trans.), New York: Oxford University Press.

Hess, Richard S., and David T. Tsumura, eds. (1994). *I Studied Inscriptions from Before the Flood: Ancient Near Eastern, Literary, and Linguistic Approaches to Genesis 1–11*, Winona Lake, IN: Eisenbrauns.

Hick, John (2010). *Evil and the Love of God*, New York: Palgrave Macmillan.

Hill, Carol A. (2000). "The Garden of Eden: A Modern Landscape," *Perspectives on Science and Christian Faith* **52**, 31–46.

Holekamp, Kay E., Laura Smale, R. Berg, and S. M. Cooper (1997). "Hunting Rates and Hunting Success in the Spotted Hyena (*Crocuta crocuta*)," *Journal of Zoology* **242**, 1–15.

Inagaki, Tristen K., and Naomi I. Eisenberger (2013). "Shared Neural Mechanisms Underlying Social Warmth and Physical Warmth," *Psychological Science* **24**, 2272–2280.

International Association for the Study of Pain (2011). "Part III: Pain Terms: A Current List with Definitions and Notes on Usage." In Harold Merskey and Nikolai Bogduk (eds.), *Classification of Chronic Pain*, 2nd ed. Online: www.iasp-pain.org/publications/free-ebooks/classification-of-chronic-pain-second-edition-revised/ (accessed August 31, 2022).

Iwaniuk, Andrew N., and John E. Nelson (2003). "Developmental Differences Are Correlated with Relative Brain Size in Birds: A Comparative Analysis," *Canadian Journal of Zoology* **81**, 1913–1928.

Jacobsen, Thorkild (1981). "The Eridu Genesis," *Journal of Biblical Literature* **100**, 513–529.

James, Michael S. (2000). "Animals Co-exist with Wildfires," *ABC News* (August 26). Online: http://abcnews.go.com/Technology/story?id=119700 (accessed August 31, 2022).

Jarvis, Erich D. (2009). "Bird Brain: Evolution." In Larry R. Squire (ed.), *Encyclopedia of Neuroscience*, Vol. 2, Oxford: Oxford Academic, pp. 209–215.

Jarvis, Erich D., Onur Güntürkün, Laura Bruce et al. (2005). "Avian Brains and A New Understanding of Vertebrate Brain Evolution," *Nature Reviews Neuroscience* **6**, 151–159.

Johnston, Philip S. (2002). *Shades of Sheol: Death and Afterlife in the Old Testament*, Downers Grove, IL: InterVarsity.

Key, Brian, Robert Arlinghaus, and Howard I. Browman (2016). "Insects Cannot Tell Us Anything about Subjective Experience of the Origin of Consciousness," *Proceedings of the National Academy of Sciences of the United States of America* **113**, E3813.

King James I. (2008). *Demonology.* Las Vegas, NV: Forgotten Books.

Kitcher, Philip (2013). "Some Answers, Admissions, and Explanations." In Marie I. Kaiser and Ansgar Seide (eds.), *Pragmatic Naturalism*, Frankfurt: Ontos Verlag, pp. 175–205.

Koenig, Harold G. (2007). "Altruistic Love and Physical Health." In Stephen G. Post (ed.), *Altruism and Health: Perspectives from Empirical Research*, New York: Oxford University Press, pp. 422–441.

Komarek, Sr., Edwin V. (1969) "Fire and Animal Behavior." In *Proceedings of the Tall Timbers Fire Ecology Conference: No.9., Tallahassee, FL*, pp. 160–207. Online: http://talltimbers.org/wp-content/uploads/2014/03/Komarek1969_op.pdf (accessed November 17, 2017).

    (1985) "Wildlife and Fire Research: Past, Present, and Future." In *USDA Forest Service General Technical Report INT-GTR-186, Ogden, UT – Intermountain Forest and Range Experiment Station* (July), pp. 1–7. Online: www.fs.usda.gov/rm/pubs_int/int_gtr186.pdf (accessed November 15, 2023).

Kuhse, Helga and Peter Singer, eds. (1999). *Bioethics: An Anthology.* Oxford: Blackwell.

Kuře, Josef, ed. (2011). *Euthanasia: The "Good Death" Controversy in Humans and Animals*, Rijeka, Croatia: InTech.

Lack, David (1947). "The Significance of Clutch-Size, Part 1," *Ibis* **89**, 302–352.

    (1948) "The Significance of Clutch-Size, Part 2," *Ibis* **90**, 25–45.

Lam, Joseph (2010). "The Biblical Creation in Its Ancient Near Eastern Context," *BioLogos website* (April 21). Online: https://biologos.org/uploads/projects/lam_scholarly_essay.pdf (accessed August 9, 2022).

Lentile, Leigh B., Frederick W. Smith, and Wayne D. Shepperd (2005). "Patch Structure, Fire-Scar Formation, and Tree Regeneration in a Large Mixed-Severity Fire in the South Dakota Black Hills, USA," *Canadian Journal of Forest Research* **35**, 2875–2885.

Lewis, Clive S. (2001). *The Problem of Pain*, New York: HarperSanFrancisco.

Lieberman, Matthew D. (2013). *Social: Why Our Brains Are Wired to Connect*, New York: Broadway Books.

Lloyd, Michael (1998). "Are Animals Fallen?" In Andrew Linzey and Dorothy Yamamoto (eds.), *Animals on the Agenda: Questions about*

Animals for Theology and Ethics, Chicago: University of Illinois Press, pp. 147–160.

Lubow, Jeffery M., Ivan G. Piñón, Angelo Avogaro et al. (2006). "Brain Oxygen Utilization Is Unchanged by Hypoglycemia in Normal Humans: Lactate, Alanine, and Leucine Uptake Are Not Sufficient to Offset Energy Deficit," *American Journal of Physiology-Endocrinology and Metabolism* 290, E149–E153.

MacLean, Paul D. (1985). "Brain Evolution Relating to Family, Play, and the Separation Call," *Archives of General Psychiatry* **42**, 405–417.

Maier, Steven F. (1989). "Determinants of the Nature of Environmentally Induced Hypoalgesia," *Behavioral Neuroscience* **103**, 131–143.

Maier, Steven F., Susan Davies, James W. Grau, et al. (1980). "Opiate Antagonists and Long-Term Analgesic Reaction Induced by Inescapable Shock in Rats," *Journal of Comparative and Physiological Psychology* **94**, 1172–1183.

Main, Douglas (2015). "Scientists Explain Video of Orca Punting a Seal 80 Feet in Air," *Newsweek* (October 29). Online: www.newsweek.com/scientists-explain-video-orca-punting-seal-80-feet-air-388554 (accessed July 26, 2022).

Mascall, Eric L. (1956). *Christian Theology and Natural Science*, New York: Ronald.

Matheson, Thomas (2002). "Invertebrate Nervous Systems." In Gina Fullerlove (ed.), *Encyclopedia of Life Sciences*, London: Nature Publishing Group, pp. 1–6.

May, Robert M. (1998). "How Many Species Are There on Earth?" *Science* **241**, 1441–1449.

McDaniel, Jay B. (1989). *Of God and Pelicans: A Theology of Reverence for Life*, Louisville, KY: Westminster/John Knox.

(1998) "Can Animal Suffering Be Reconciled with Belief in an All-Loving God?" In Andrew Linzey and Dorothy Yamamoto (eds.), *Animals on the Agenda: Questions about Animals for Theology and Ethics*, Chicago: University of Illinois Press, pp. 161–170.

Melzack, Ronald, and Stephen G. Dennis (1978). "Neurophysiological Foundations of Pain." In Richard A. Sternbach (ed.), *The Psychology of Pain*, New York: Raven, pp. 1–26.

Middleton, J. Richard (2017). "Reading Genesis 3 Attentive to Human Evolution." In *Evolution and the Fall*, William T. Cavanaugh and James K. Smith (eds.), Grand Rapids, MI: Eerdmans, pp. 67–97.

Miller, Kenneth R. (2007). *Finding Darwin's God: A Scientist's Search for Common Ground between God and Evolution*, New York: Harper Perennial.

Miller, Michael W., Heather M. Swanson, Lisa L. Wolfe et al. (2008). "Lions and Prions and Deer Demise," *PLoS ONE* **3**, e4019.

Moberly, R. Walter L. (1988). "Did the Serpent Get It Right?" *Journal of Theological Studies* **39**, 1–27.

Mock, Douglas W. (1984). "Infanticide, Siblicide, and Avian Nestling Mortality." In Glenn Hausfater and Sarah B. Hrdy (eds.), *Infanticide: Comparative and Evolutionary Perspectives*, New York: Aldine, pp. 3–30.

Mock, Douglas W., Hugh Drummond, and Christopher H. Stinson (1990). "Avian Siblicide," *American Scientist* **78**, 438–449.

Molina, Patricia E. (2003). "Endogenous Opioid Analgesia in Hemorrhagic Shock," *Journal of Trauma-Injury Infection and Critical Care* **54**, 126–132.

(2006). "Opioids and Opiates: Analgesia with Cardiovascular, Haemodynamic and Immune Implications in Critical Illness," *Journal of Internal Medicine* **259**, 138–154.

Moritz, Joshua M. (2014). "Animal Suffering, Evolution, and the Origins of Evil: Toward a 'Free Creatures' Defense," *Zygon* **49**, 348–380.

Mosley, Craig (2011). "Pain and Nociception in Reptiles," *Analgesia and Pain Management* **14**, 45–60.

Murray, Michael J. (2011). *Nature Red in Tooth and Claw: Theism and the Problem of Animal Suffering*, Oxford: Oxford University Press.

Newton, Ian (1977). "Breeding Strategies in Birds of Prey," *Living Bird* **16**, 51–82.

Oden, Thomas C. (1992). *Classical Christianity: A Systematic Theology*, New York: HarperOne.

Osborn, Ronald E. (2014). *Death Before the Fall: Biblical Literalism and the Problem of Animal Suffering*, Downers Grove, IL: IVP Academic.

Page, Ruth (1996). *God and the Web of Creation*. London: SCM.

Panksepp, Jaak, Barbara H. Herman, R. Conner, P. Bishop, and J. P. Scott (1978). "The Biology of Social Attachments: Opiates Alleviate Separation Distress," *Biological Psychiatry* **13**, 607–618.

Panksepp, Jaak, Barbara H. Herman, Thomas Vilberg, P. Bishop, and Fatima G. DeEskinazi (1980). "Endogenous Opioids and Social Behavior," *Neuroscience and Behavioral Reviews* **4**, 473–487.

Peacocke, Arthur (1993). *Theology for a Scientific Age: Being and Becoming – Natural, Divine, and Human*, Minneapolis, MN: Fortress.

(2001) "The Cost of New Life." In John Polkinghorne (ed.), *The Work of Love: Creation as Kenosis*, Grand Rapids, MI: Eerdmans, pp. 21–42.

Peterson, Michael, William Hasker, Bruce Reichenbach, and David Basinger (2009). *Reason and Religious Belief: An Introduction to the Philosophy of Religion*, 4th ed., New York: Oxford University Press.

Pinnock, Clark H. (2001). *Most Moved Mover: A Theology of God's Openness*, Carlisle: Paternoster.

Plantinga, Alvin (2011). *Where the Conflict Really Lies: Science, Religion, and Naturalism*, Oxford: Oxford University Press.

Plotnik, Joshua M. (2014). "Asian Elephants *(Elephas maximus)* Reassure Others in Distress," *PeerJ* **2**, e278.

Poinar, Jr., George, and Roberta Poinar (2008). *What Bugged the Dinosaurs?: Insects, Disease, and Death in the Cretaceous*, Princeton, NJ: Princeton University Press.

Polkinghorne, John (2004). *Science and the Trinity: The Christian Encounter with Reality*, New Haven, CT: Yale University Press.

(2010) "The Universe as Creation." In Michael Peterson, William Hasker, Bruce Reichenbach, and David Basinger (eds.), *Philosophy of Religion: Selected Readings*, 4th ed., New York: Oxford University Press, pp. 551–559.

Polkinghorne, John, ed. (2001). *The Work of Love: Creation as Kenosis*, Grand Rapids, MI: Eerdmans.

Price, Theodore J., and Gregory Dussor (2014). "Evolution: The Advantage of 'Maladaptive' Pain Plasticity," *Current Biology* **24**, R384–R386.

Rainville, Pierre, Gary H. Duncan, Donald D. Price, Benoît Carrier, and Mary Catherine Bushnell (1997). "Pain Affect Encoded in Human Anterior Cingulate but Not Somatosensory Cortex," *Science* **277**, 968–971.

Reece, Jane B., Martha R. Taylor, Eric J. Simon, and Jean L. Dickey (2011). *Campbell Biology: Concepts and Connections*, 7th ed., New York: Pearson.

Reeder, DeeAnn M., and Kristin M. Kramer (2005). "Stress in Free-Ranging Mammals: Integrating Physiology, Ecology, and Natural History," *Journal of Mammalogy* **86**, 225–235.

Rivat, Cyril, Emilie Laboureyras, Jean-Paul Laulin et al. (2007). "Non-nociceptive Environmental Stress Induces Hyperalgesia, Not Analgesia, in Pain and Opioid-Experienced Rats," *Neuropsychopharmacology* **32**, 2217–2228.

Robbins, Frank Egleston (1912). "The Influence of Greek Philosophy on the Early Commentaries of Genesis," *American Journal of Theology* **16**, 218–240.

Rollin, Bernard E. (2009). "Ethics and Euthanasia," *Canadian Veterinary Journal* **50**, 1081–1086.

Rolston III, Holmes (1987). *Science and Religion: A Critical Survey*, Philadelphia, PA: Temple University Press.

(2003) "Naturalizing and Systematizing Evil." In Willem B. Drees (ed.), *Is Nature Ever Evil? Religion, Science, and Value*, London: Routledge, pp. 67–86.

Rose, James D., Robert Arlinghaus, Steven J. Cooke et al. (2014). "Can Fish Really Feel Pain?" *Fish and Fisheries* **15**, 97–133.

Rowe, William L. (1979). "The Problem of Evil and Some Varieties of Atheism," *American Philosophical Quarterly* **16**, 335–341.

Sauer, James A. (1996). "The River Runs Dry: Creation Story Preserves Historical Memory," *Biblical Archaeology Review* **22**, 52–57, 64.

Scheiber, Isabella B. R., Brigitte M. Weiß, Sjouke A. Kingma, and Jan Komdeur (2017). "The Importance of the Altricial-Precocial Spectrum for Social Complexity in Mammals and Birds: A Review," *Frontiers in Zoology* **14**, 3. Online: https://frontiersinzoology.biomedcentral.com/articles/10.1186/s12983-016-0185-6 (accessed November 15, 2023).

Schneider, John R. (2020). *Animal Suffering and the Darwinian Problem of Evil*, New York: Cambridge University Press.

Schurr, Avital (2006). "Lactate: The Ultimate Cerebral Oxidative Energy Substrate," *Journal of Cerebral Blood Flow and Metabolism* **26**, 142–152.

Sharim, J., and N. Pouratian (2016). "Anterior Cingulotomy for the Treatment of Chronic Intractable Pain: A Systematic Review," *Pain Physician Journal* **19**, 537–550.

Smith, Douglas W., and Gary Ferguson (2005). *Decade of the Wolf: Returning the Wild to Yellowstone*, Guilford, CT: Lyons Press.

Smith, Jane A. (1991). "A Question of Pain in Invertebrates," *Institute for Laboratory Animals Journal* **33**, 25–31.

Sollereder, Bethany N. (2019). *God, Evolution, and Animal Suffering: Theodicy Without a Fall*, New York: Routledge.

Southgate, Christopher (2008). *The Groaning of Creation: God, Evolution, and the Problem of Evil*. Louisville, KY: Westminster John Knox.

Starck, J. Matthais (1993). "Evolution of Avian Ontogenies," *Current Ornithology* **10**, 275–366.

State Government of Victoria, Australia (2014). "Shock," Department of Health website. Online: www.betterhealth.vic.gov.au/health/conditionsandtreatments/shock (accessed July 15, 2022).

Talbot, Jeanne D., Sean Marrett, Alan C. Evans et al. (1991). "Multiple Representations of Pain in Human Cerebral Cortex," *Science* **251**, 1355–1358.

Tooley, Michael (2019). *The Problem of Evil*, New York: Cambridge University Press.

Towler, Dwight A., Carolyn E. Havlin, Suzanne Craft, and Philip Cryer (1993). "Mechanism of Awareness of Hypoglycemia. Perception of Neurogenic (Predominantly Cholinergic) Rather than Neuroglycopenic Symptoms," *Diabetes* **42**, 1791–1798.

Trethowan, Illtyd (1954). *An Essay in Christian Philosophy*, London: Longmans, Green & Co.

Tsevat, Matitiahu (1980). "The Meaning of the Book of Job." In *The Meaning of the Book of Job and Other Biblical Studies: Essays on the Literature and Religion of the Hebrew Bible*, New York: Ktav, pp. 1–37.

Tsumura, David (2005). *Creation and Destruction: A Reappraisal of the Chaoskampf Theory in the Old Testament*, Winona Lake, IN: Eisenbrauns.

Ugolino di Monte Santa Maria (1998). *Little Flowers of St. Francis*, Christian Classics Ethereal Library, W. Heywood (trans.), New York: Vintage Books, Chapter 16. Online: https://ccel.org/ccel/ugolino/flowers/flowers.iii.xvi.html (accessed August 31, 2022).

University of Miami (2018). "Predatory Behavior of Great White Sharks," Shark Research website. Online: https://sharkresearch.rsmas.miami.edu/research/projects/great-white-predation (accessed July 15, 2022).

University of Utah (2010). "How Cells Communicate During Fight or Flight" (September 2), Genetic Science Learning Center website. Online: http://learn.genetics.utah.edu/content/cells/fight_flight/ (accessed August 31, 2022).

U.S. National Academy of Sciences (USNAS) (2009). *Recognition and Alleviation of Pain in Animals*, Washington, DC: National Academies Press.

U.S. National Park Service (2017). "Video: Living with Fire in the Grand Canyon," U.S. National Park Service website (April 24). Online: www.nps.gov/media/video/view.htm?id=3A09C7DC-1DD8-B71B-0B409785F7F0A07C (accessed July 14, 2022).

Venema, Dennis R., and Scot McKnight (2017). *Adam and the Genome: Reading Scripture after Genetic Science*, Grand Rapids, MI: Brazos.

Viney, Donald (2018). "Process Theism." In Edward N. Zalta (ed.), *The Stanford Encyclopedia of Philosophy* (Summer 2018 Edition). Online: https://plato.stanford.edu/entries/process-theism/ (accessed January 22, 2020).

Visser, Ingrid N., Olle G. L. Carlsson, Santiago Imberti et al. (2008). "Antarctic Peninsula Killer Whales (*Orcinus orca*) Hunt Seals and a Penguin on Floating Ice," *Marine Mammal Science* **24**, 225–234.

Vogl, Richard J. (1973). "Effects of Fire on the Plants and Animals of a Florida Wetland," *The American Midland Naturalist* **89**, 334–347.

von Rad, Gerhard (1961). *Genesis*, Old Testament Library, John H. Marks (trans.), Philadelphia, PA: Westminster.

Waal, Frans de (2013). *The Bonobo and the Atheist: In Search of Humanism Among the Primates*, New York: W. W. Norton.

Wager, Tor D., Lauren Y. Atlas, Martin A. Lindquist et al. (2013). "An fMRI-Based Neurologic Signature of Physical Pain," *The New England Journal of Medicine* **368**, 1388–1397.

Walton, John H. (1990). *Ancient Israelite Literature in Its Cultural Context: A Survey of Parallels between Biblical and Ancient Near Eastern Texts*, Grand Rapids, MI: Zondervan.

(2009). *The Lost World of Genesis One: Ancient Cosmology and the Origins Debate*, Downers Grove, IL: InterVarsity.

(2011) *Genesis 1 as Ancient Cosmology*, Winona Lake, IN: Eisenbrauns.

(2018) *Ancient Near Eastern Thought and the Old Testament: Introducing the Conceptual World of the Hebrew Bible*, 2nd ed., Grand Rapids, MI: BakerAcademic.

Watkins, Linda R., and David J. Mayer (1982). "Organization of Endogenous Opiate and Nonopiate Pain Control Systems," *Science* **216**, 1185–1192.

Wenham, Gordon J. (1994) "Sanctuary Symbolism in the Garden of Eden Story." In Richard S. Hess and David T. Tsumura (eds.), *I Studied Inscriptions from Before the Flood: Ancient Near Eastern, Literary, and Linguistic Approaches to Genesis 1–11*, Winona Lake, IN: Eisenbrauns, pp. 399–404.

(2014) *Genesis 1–15*. Word Biblical Commentary 1, Grand Rapids, Mich.: Zondervan.

Werther, David, and Mark D. Linville, eds. (2012). *Philosophy and the Christian Worldview: Analysis, Assessment and Development*, New York: Continuum International.

Wesley, John (1872). "The General Deliverance." Sermon 60 in *The Sermons of John Wesley*, Thomas Jackson (ed.), Wesley Center Online website. Online: http://wesley.nnu.edu/john-wesley/the-sermons-of-john-wesley-1872-edition/sermon-60-the-general-deliverance/ (accessed August 31, 2022).

Westermann, Claus (1994). *Genesis 1–11*, Continental Commentaries, John J. Scullion (trans.), Minneapolis, MN: Fortress.

White, Joël, Sarah Leclaire, Marion Kriloff et al. (2010). "Sustained Increase in Food Supplies Reduces Broodmate Aggression in Black-Legged Kittiwakes," *Animal Behaviour* **79**, 1095–1100.

White, Lois, Gena Duncan, and Wendy Baumle (2013). *Medical Surgical Nursing: An Integrated Approach*, 3rd ed., Clifton, NY: Delmar Cengage Learning.

Wiebe, Karen L., and Gary R. Bortolotti (2000). "Parental Interference in Sibling Aggression in Birds: What Should We Look For?" *Ecoscience* **7**, 1–9.

Wiley, Tatha (2002). *Original Sin: Origins, Developments, Contemporary Meanings*, New York: Paulist.

Winnie, Jr., John, and Scott Creel (2017). "The Many Effects of Carnivores on Their Prey and Their Implications for Trophic Cascades, and Ecosystem Structure and Function," *Food Webs* **12**, 88–94.

Witherington III, Ben (2006). *New Testament History: A Narrative Account*, Grand Rapids, MI: BakerAcademic.

Wolde, Ellen van (2015). "'Creation Out of Nothing' and the Hebrew Bible." In *Creation Stories in Dialogue: The Bible, Science, and Folk Traditions*, Biblical Interpretation Series 139, Alan Culpepper and Jan G. van der Watt (eds.), Leiden: Brill, pp. 157–176.

Wolff, Hans W. (1981). *Anthropology of the Old Testament*, M. Kohl (trans.), London: SCM Press.

Cambridge Elements ≡

The Problems of God

Series Editor

Michael L. Peterson
Asbury Theological Seminary

Michael L. Peterson is Professor of Philosophy at Asbury Theological Seminary. He is the author of *God and Evil* (Routledge); *Monotheism, Suffering, and Evil* (Cambridge University Press); *With All Your Mind* (University of Notre Dame Press); *C. S. Lewis and the Christian Worldview* (Oxford University Press); *Evil and the Christian God* (Baker Book House); and *Philosophy of Education: Issues and Options* (Intervarsity Press). He is coauthor of *Reason and Religious Belief* (Oxford University Press); *Science, Evolution, and Religion: A Debate about Atheism and Theism* (Oxford University Press); and *Biology, Religion, and Philosophy* (Cambridge University Press). He is editor of *The Problem of Evil: Selected Readings* (University of Notre Dame Press). He is coeditor of *Philosophy of Religion: Selected Readings* (Oxford University Press) and *Contemporary Debates in Philosophy of Religion* (Wiley-Blackwell). He served as General Editor of the Blackwell monograph series Exploring Philosophy of Religion and is founding Managing Editor of the journal *Faith and Philosophy*.

About the Series

This series explores problems related to God, such as the human quest for God or gods, contemplation of God, and critique and rejection of God. Concise, authoritative volumes in this series will reflect the methods of a variety of disciplines, including philosophy of religion, theology, religious studies, and sociology.

Cambridge Elements ≡

The Problems of God

Printed in the United States
by Baker & Taylor Publisher Services